HEALTH & WELLNESS

EDITED BY GAYLE M. WELLS

SECOND EDITION

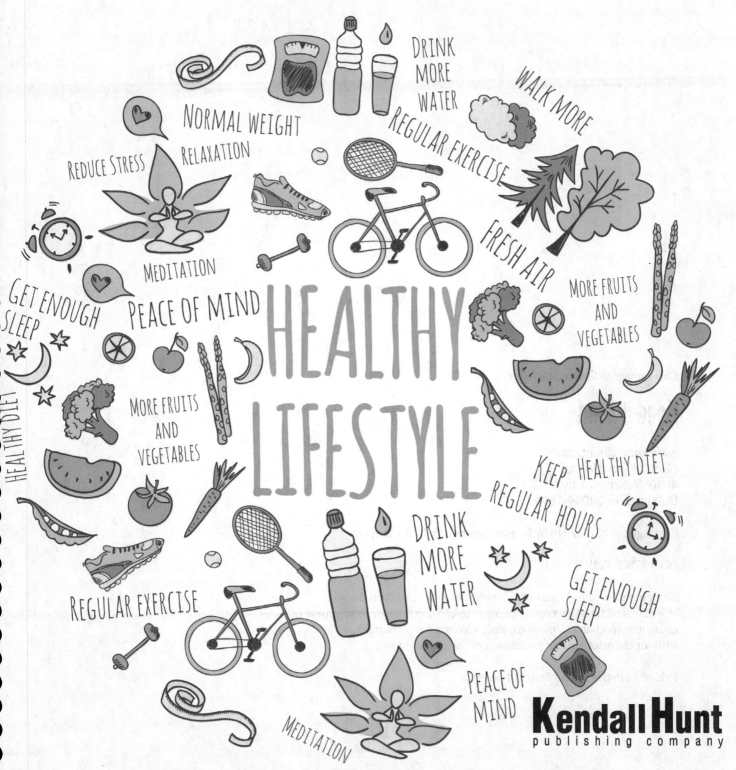

Kendall Hunt publishing company

Cover image © Shutterstock, Inc.

Kendall Hunt
publishing company

www.kendallhunt.com
Send all inquiries to:
4050 Westmark Drive
Dubuque, IA 52004-1840

Copyright © 2017, 2018 by Kendall Hunt Publishing Company

ISBN 978-1-5249-7002-4

Published in the United States of America

TABLE OF CONTENTS

HEALTHY LIFESTYLE

© Martin Kalimon/Shutterstock.com

ACKNOWLEDGMENTS

Teaching and learning often works best with a team approach, and this book is a product of several teams working in tandem. We have been fortunate to work with an encouraging team at Kendall Hunt Publishing. Their support and creativity made this project run smoothly. We are also grateful for the support of professionals at Western Carolina University who are committed to health and wellness as a core academic experience for all students. Moreover, this project would not have been possible without the committed health and physical educators who contributed their ideas, time, and expertise. Special thanks to the following colleagues at Western Carolina University who contributed to this text.

Bob Beaudet
Associate Professor of Health and Physical Education

Chelsea Burrell
Graduate Student; Adjunct Faculty

Leigh Hilger
Instructor of Health

Sarah Lowell
Retired K-12 Physical Educator; Adjunct Faculty

Aubrey Ray
PhD Student; Adjunct Faculty

Debby Singleton
Instructor of Parks and Recreation Management

Alyssa Sinyard
Instructor of Health

Heidi Turlington
Instructor of Health

Introduction

When you signed up for health and wellness, you probably thought you would be learning about physical fitness and nutrition. You are right! Wellness incorporates both fitness and nutrition. However, these topics are only a small part of the big picture concept of wellness. In this chapter, you will be learning about the idea of wellness and the different dimensions we must strive to maintain during our lives.

Each of the different dimensions of wellness, including *physical, emotional, social, intellectual, environmental*, and *spiritual*, plays an important role in our overall well-being. However, each dimension also impacts the other dimensions. For example, practicing good physical fitness and nutritional habits helps to reduce your risk for developing chronic diseases. Fitness activities can also boost your emotional well-being and provide opportunities to interact socially. If you are experiencing an emotional disorder, such as depression, it may affect your social, physical, and spiritual choices. If there is a pollutant in the environment, exposure can affect your physical wellness. Therefore, it is important that we learn to value and balance all of these dimensions.

After you graduate from college, your health and wellness will impact your ability to do your job well, enjoy time with family and friends, learn how to do new activities, and relate to the world around you. When you think about it that way, wellness is important to every aspect of our lives! But wellness does not just happen without effort over time. As you get older, a lot of illnesses are a result of years of bad habits. Wellness requires purposeful development of good strategies that will help you be healthy now and maintain wellness in the future. In this chapter, you will assess your current wellness, think about areas for improvement, and strategize for making healthy habits that will impact your wellness for a lifetime.

© bleakstar/Shutterstock.com

Contributed by Heidi Turlington. Copyright © Kendall Hunt Publishing Company.

Wellness Questionnaire

Name _____   **Date** _____

The purpose of this questionnaire is to analyze current lifestyle habits and help determine changes necessary for future health and wellness. Check the appropriate answer to each question and obtain a final score according to the guidelines provided at the end of the questionnaire.

Course _____   Section _____

Gender _____   Age _____

	Always	Nearly Always	Often	Seldom	Never
1. I participate in vigorous aerobic activity for 20 minutes on three of more days per week, and I accumulate at least 30 minutes of moderate-intensity physical activity on a minimum of three additional days per week.	☐	☐	☐	☐	☐
2. I participate in strength-training exercises, using a minimum of eight different exercises, two or more days per week.	☐	☐	☐	☐	☐
3. I perform flexibility exercises a minimum of three days per week.	☐	☐	☐	☐	☐
4. I maintain recommended body weight (includes avoidance of excessive body fat, excessive thinness, or frequent fluctuations in body weight).	☐	☐	☐	☐	☐
5. Every day, I eat three regular meals that include a wide variety of foods.	☐	☐	☐	☐	☐
6. I limit the amount of fat and saturated fat in my diet on most days of the week.	☐	☐	☐	☐	☐
7. I eat a minimum of five servings of fruits and vegetables and six servings from grain products daily.	☐	☐	☐	☐	☐
8. I regularly avoid snacks, especially those that are high in calories and fat and low in nutrients and fiber.	☐	☐	☐	☐	☐
9. I avoid cigarettes or tobacco in any other form.	☐	☐	☐	☐	☐
10. I avoid alcoholic beverages. If I drink, I do so in moderation (one daily drink for women and two for men), and I do not combine alcohol with other drugs.	☐	☐	☐	☐	☐
11. I avoid additive drugs and needles that have been used by others.	☐	☐	☐	☐	☐
12. I use prescription drugs and over-the-counter drugs sparingly, only when needed, and I follow all directions for their proper use.	☐	☐	☐	☐	☐

	Always	Nearly Always	Often	Seldom	Never
13. I readily recognize when I am under excessive tension and stress (distress).	☐	☐	☐	☐	☐
14. I am able to perform effective stress-management techniques.	☐	☐	☐	☐	☐
15. I have close friends and relatives with whom I can discuss personal problems and approach for help when needed, and with whom I can express my feelings freely.	☐	☐	☐	☐	☐
16. I spend most of my daily leisure time in wholesome recreational activities.	☐	☐	☐	☐	☐
17. I sleep 7 to 8 hours each night.	☐	☐	☐	☐	☐
18. I floss my teeth every day and brush them at least twice daily.	☐	☐	☐	☐	☐
19. I avoid overexposure to the sun, and I use sunscreen and appropriate clothing when I am out in the sun for an extended time.	☐	☐	☐	☐	☐
20. I avoid using products that have not been shown by science to be safe and effective (this includes anabolic steroids and unproven nutrient and weight loss supplements).	☐	☐	☐	☐	☐
21. I stay current with the warning signs for heart attack, stroke, and cancer.	☐	☐	☐	☐	☐
22. I practice monthly breast/testicle self-exams, get recommended screening tests (blood lipids, blood pressure, Pap test), and seek a medical evaluation when I am not well or disease symptoms arise.	☐	☐	☐	☐	☐
23. I have a dental checkup at least once a year, and I get regular medical exams according to age recommendations.	☐	☐	☐	☐	☐
24. I am not sexually active/I practice safe sex.	☐	☐	☐	☐	☐
25. I can deal effectively with disappointments and temporary feelings for sadness, loneliness, and depression. If I am unable to deal with these feelings, I seek professional help.	☐	☐	☐	☐	☐
26. I can work out emotional problems without turning to alcohol or other drugs.	☐	☐	☐	☐	☐
27. I associate with people who have a positive attitude about life.	☐	☐	☐	☐	☐
28. I respond to temporary setbacks by making the best of the circumstances and by moving ahead with optimism and energy. I do not spend time and talent worrying about failures.	☐	☐	☐	☐	☐

29. I wear a seatbelt whenever I am in a car, I ask other in my vehicle to do the same, and I make sure that children are in an infant seat or wear a shoulder harness. ☐ ☐ ☐ ☐ ☐

30. I do not drive under the influence of alcohol or other drugs, and I make an effort to keep others from doing the same. ☐ ☐ ☐ ☐ ☐

31. I avoid being alone in public places, especially after dark; I seek escorts when I visit or exercise in unfamiliar places. ☐ ☐ ☐ ☐ ☐

32. I seek to make my living quarters accident-free, and I keep doors and windows locked, especially when I am home alone. ☐ ☐ ☐ ☐ ☐

33. I try to minimize environmental pollutants, and I support community efforts to minimize pollution. ☐ ☐ ☐ ☐ ☐

34. I keep my living quarters clean and organized. ☐ ☐ ☐ ☐ ☐

35. I study and/or work in a clean environment (including avoidance of second-hand smoke). ☐ ☐ ☐ ☐ ☐

36. I participate in recycling programs for paper, cardboard, glass, plastic, and aluminum ☐ ☐ ☐ ☐ ☐

How to Score:

Enter a score for each question in the space provided below. Always=5, Nearly always=4, Often=3, Seldom=2, and Never=1. Next, total the score for each specific wellness lifestyle category and obtain a rating for each category according to the criteria provided below.

	Health Related Fitness	Nutrition	Avoiding Chemical Dependency	Stress Management	Personal Hygiene/ Health	Disease Prevention	Emotional Well-being	Personal Safety	Environmental Health & Protection
	1)	5)	S)	13)	17)	21)	25)	29)	33)
	2)	6)	10)	14)	18)	22)	26)	30)	34)
	3)	7)	11)	16)	19)	23)	27)	31)	35)
	4)	8)	12)	16)	20)	24)	28)	32)	36)
Total									
Rating									

Source: Health and Physical Education Program at Western Carolina University. Reprinted with permission.

Category Rating:

Excellent (E) =>17 Your answers show that you are aware of the importance of this category to your health and wellness. You are putting your knowledge to work for you by practicing good habits. As long as you continue to do so, this category should not pose a health risk. You are also setting a good example for family and friends to follow. Because you got a very high test score on this part of the test, you may want to consider other categories in which your score indicates room for improvement.

Good (G) =13 – 16 You health practices in this area are good, but you have room for improvement. Look again at the items you answered with a Seldom or Never and identify changes that you can make to improve your lifestyle. Even small changes often can help you achieve better health.

Needs Improvement (NI) =<12 Your health risks are showing. You may be taking serious and unnecessary risks with your health. Perhaps you are not aware of the risks and what to do about them. Most likely you need additional information and help in deciding how to successfully make the changes you desire. You can easily get the information that you need to improve, if you wish. The next step is up to you.

Please note that no final overall rating is provided for the entire questionnaire, because it may not be indicative of your overall wellness. For example, an excellent rating in most categories will not offset the immediate health risks and life-threatening consequences of using additive drugs or not wearing a seatbelt.

Group Members: _____

Wellness Scavenger Hunt

Directions: In this chapter, we learn about the domains of wellness: mental, physical, emotional, environmental, social, and spiritual. Find each location and take a group pic (your group must stay together). Then, identify the area of wellness for each location. Everybody should wear a pedometer on the scavenger hunt. When you get back, you will record your number of steps.

Location	Pic	Wellness dimensions (mental, physical, emotional, environmental, social, and spiritual)
1. Campus Recreation Center(CRC)	Your group doing yoga poses	
2. Health Center	On the Bird Building steps	
3. Counseling Center	Bulletin board outside the counseling center	
4. Library	Your favorite studying pose	
5. Hillside Grind Coffeehouse	By the Hillside Grind sign	
6. Writing and Learning Commons (WaLC)	By the WaLC sign	
Bonus: Find something that needs to be recycled. (1 point for each item)	Take a pic of someone in your group placing the item in a recycling container (up to five items)	

Source: Health and Physical Education Program at Western Carolina University. Reprinted with permission.

Health Fitness Test Data Sheet

Please use pen or write darkly

Name: _____

92#: _____ Gender: _____ Age: _____

- **Circle Class:**   Freshman   Sophomore   Junior   Senior
- **Fill in your section number:**   Health 123 _____   OR   Health 111 _____
- **PRE Test Date:** _____   POST Test Date: _____
- **Circle Semester:**   FALL   SPRING   MAY   MINI   SUMMER 1   SUMMER 2

(Tests # 1, 2, and 3 must be completed before exercise.) (PRE= beginning of semester; POST = end of semester)

1. Blood Pressure (Systolic/Diastolic)   **2. Pulse or RHR** (BPM)

PRE_____/_____ POST_____/_____   PRE_____ POST_____
    Systolic   Diastolic   Systolic   Diastolic   BPM   BPM

1. Blood Pressure (mm Hg)		
Category	Systolic	Diastolic
Normal	<120	<80
Prehypertensive	121-139	81-89
Stage 1 Hypertension	140-159	90-99
Stage 2 Hypertension	>160	>100

2. Pulse or Resting Heart Rate	
Beats per Minute	Rating
≤ 59	Excellent
60-69	Good
70-79	Average
80-89	Fair
>90	Poor

3. Body Composition
(Must be completed before exercise.)

	PRE	POST
Height (inches) (shoes off)	_____	_____
Weight (pounds) (shoes off)	_____	_____
% Body Fat	_____	_____
BMI (Body Mass Index)	_____	_____

% Body Fat	MEN	WOMEN
Essential Fat	3-5%	8-12%
Minimal	5 %	10-12%
Athletic	5-13%	12-22%
Recommended	8-22%	20-35%
Obese	>23%	>36%
*standards for < or equal to 34 years old		

BMI	Less than 18.5 Underweight
	18.5 to 24.9 Normal
	25 to 29.9 Overweight
	Equal to or over 30 Obese

4. Step Test
(Cardio-respiratory Endurance)
Recovery Heart Rate
Step up & down for 3 minutes, 12" bench, 24 steps per minute (96bpm). Once completed, sit down on bench, count HR for one minute, start with "zero".

PRE_____ POST_____

Age 18 to 25	Excellent	Good	Average	Poor	Needs Attention
Women	72-83	88–97	100-124	128–137	138+
Men	70-78	82-88	91-114	118-126	127+

5. Abdominal Endurance
Number of sit-ups in one minute. Arms across chest. Touch elbows to mid-thigh. Shoulder blades must touch mat each time.

PRE_____ POST_____

	MEN			Women	
%ile	<20 yr	20-29yr	%ile	<20 yr	20-29yr
90	55	52	90	54	49
80	51	47	80	46	44
70	48	45	70	38	41
60	47	42	60	36	38
50	45	40	50	34	35
40	41	38	40	32	32
30	38	35	30	29	30
20	36	33	20	28	27
10	33	30	10	25	23

6. Upper Body Endurance
Number of push-ups without resting or stopping.
Women use modified style. Men use regular pushup and lower to partner's fist under chest.

PRE_____ POST_____

	MEN			Women	
%ile	<20yr	20-29yr	%il e	<20yr	20-29yr
90	57	46	90	42	36
80	47	39	80	36	31
70	41	34	70	32	28
60	37	30	60	30	24
50	33	27	50	26	21
40	29	24	40	23	19
30	26	20	30	20	15
20	22	17	20	17	11
10	18	13	10	12	8

7. Sit and Reach Flexibility

Best of 3 tries in inches. Measures flexibility of hamstrings & lower back. (Use numbers in "circles" on sit-reach box.)

Best PRE:_____ Best POST:_____
(Record score in inches.)

	MEN			Women	
%ile	<20yr	20-29yr	%ile	<20yr	20-29yr
90	22.6	21.8	90	24.3	23.8
80	22.5	20.5	80	22.5	22.5
70	22.0	19.5	70	22.0	21.5
60	21.5	18.5	60	21.5	20.5
50	18	17.5	50	21.0	20.0
40	16.5	16.5	40	20.5	19.3
30	15.5	15.5	30	19.5	18.3
20	13.2	14.4	20	18.5	17.0
10	10.5	12.3	10	14.5	15.4

8. Shoulder Reach Flexibility

One arm up, other down, reach for fingers. Average of 2 measurements. (distance between or overlap of fingers)
R elbow up **PRE**: _____ R elbow up **POST**: _____
L elbow up **PRE**: _____ L elbow up **POST**: _____

Average of 2 **PRE**: _____ Average of 2 **POST**: _____

Rating	Average of 2 sides in inches
Excellent	> or = 5"
Above Average	2" to 4.75"
Average	0 to 1.75"
Below Average	-1 to -0.25"
Poor	< -1 "

Source: Health and Physical Education Program at Western Carolina University. Reprinted with permission.

Behavior Change Project Brainstorming

1. Think about the dimensions of wellness. List some areas that people might need to change in each of the dimensions.

   Physical: Emotional:

   Social: Environmental:

   Spiritual: Intellectual:

2. Think about the wellness assessments you have been completing. What is one area that you would like to improve?

3. Why do you want to change this area? How is this negatively impacting your health and wellness?

4. What short- and long-term benefits to your health and wellness do you hope to see by the end of your project?

5. Now we will begin to set a goal for your project. A SMART goal is specific, measurable, achievable, realistic, and time bound. For example, "I plan to lose 4–8 pounds in the next 4 weeks." You can measure that by getting on a scale, it is healthy and realistic to lose 1–2 pounds a week, and you have a deadline of 4 weeks. Write your SMART goal below:

6. Next you will need some specific strategies, or objectives, to help you meet your goal. What are the three specific things you can do that will help you meet your goal? For example, in the weight loss goal, an objective would be to do cardiovascular activity 30 min five times a week.

Source: Health and Physical Education Program at Western Carolina University. Reprinted with permission.

Health 123: Body Composition Assessment   **Name:** _____

Instructions: Choose a partner to help you complete measurements. Each person will calculate body composition using a variety of methods.

Station 1: Body Mass Index

1. Measure height in inches with shoes off _____

2. Measure weight in pounds _____

3. Using your text, determine your body mass index (BMI) by looking up the number where your weight and height intersect on the table.

   BMI = _____ Classification (e.g., underweight, normal, and overweight)_____

4. Using a regular tape measure, find your waist circumference in inches. Measure above the hip bones at the most narrow point in your waist.

   Waist circumference in inches = _____

5. Use Table 7-2 on page 252 in your text to determine your disease risk based on your BMI and waist circumference.

   Disease risk (e.g., none, increased, and high) = _____

Station 2: Percent of Body Fat Using Bioelectrical Impedance

1. **Bioelectrical Impedance**

   Input your height, weight, age, and gender into the BIA. Press START. Write down the percent body fat (%bf) measurement it displays.

   %bf based on BIA = _____

Station 2: Body Fat Classification

1. **Classification:** Using Figure 7-9 on page 254 in your text book, how would you classify your %bf (e.g., minimal, athletic, and recommended).

   Classification based on %bf = _____

   Source: Health and Physical Education Program at Western Carolina University. Reprinted with permission.

Station 3: Percent of Body Fat Using Measurements

MEN use this method.

1. Using a regular tape measure, determine the following girth measurements in *inches*.

    Waist: measure at belly button _____

    Wrist: measure in front of the bones where the wrist bends _____

2. Subtract the wrist measurement from the waist measurement.
    Waist _____ – Wrist _____ = _____.

3. Subject's body weight (BW) in pounds = _____.

4. Look up the %bf in the table by using the difference obtained in step 2 above the person's BW.

5. **%bf = _____.**

** WOMEN use this method.**

1. Using a regular tape measure, determine the following girth measurements in *centimeters*.

    Upper arm: Measure the girth halfway between the shoulder and the elbow _____

    Hip: Measure at the point of largest circumference _____

    Wrist: Take the girth in front of the bones where the wrist bends _____

2. Subject's age = _____.

3. Using the following table, find the girth measurement for each site in the left-hand columns. Look up the constant values in the right-hand columns. These values will allow you to derive body density (BD) by substituting the constants in the following formula: BD = A – B – C + D, where A = arm, B = age, C = hip, and D = wrist.

Arm (cm) =	Constant A =
Age =	Constant B =
Hip (cm) =	Constant C =
Wrist (cm) =	Constant D =

BD = A – B – C + D.

BD = _____.

4. Using the derived BD, calculate %bf according to the following equation:

    %bf = (495/BD) – 450.

    %bf = (495/ _____) – 450 = _____.

Station 4: Waist Circumference (Body Fat Distribution)

1. Measure your waist at the smallest point. For best results, have a partner measure your waist while standing at your side; be sure to keep the measuring tape flat against your skin and parallel to the ground. Record the measurement:

   Waist circumference in inches = _____.

2. Find your rating in the table on page 267. Record it here

   Rating: _____.

Station 5: Waist-to-Hip Ratio (Body Fat Distribution)

1. Use your waist circumference measurement from station 4: _____ inches.

2. Measure your hips at the widest point. For best results, have a partner measure your hip circumference while standing at your side; keep the measuring tape flat against your skin and parallel to the ground.

   Hip circumference in inches = _____.

3. Calculate your ratio by dividing your waist circumference by your hip circumference; make sure both measurements are in inches.

   Waist-to-hip ratio = waist circumference _____ ÷ hip circumference_____ = _____.

4. Find your rating in the table on page 268.

   Waist-to-hip ratio rating: _____.

Waist-to-Height Ratio (Body Fat Distribution)

1. Use waist circumference measurement from station 4: _____ inches.

2. Measure height with shoes off in inches

   Height in inches: _____

3. Calculate your ratio by dividing your waist circumference by your height; make sure both measurements are in inches

   Waist-to-height ratio= waist circumference _____ ÷ height _____ = _____

4. If your ratio is 0.5 or less, record a rating of *OK*; if your ratio is above 0.5, record a rating of *increased risk*:

   Waist-to-height ratio rating: _____.

Recommended Body Weight Using Percent Body Fat

1. Determine the pounds of BW that are fat (FW) by multiplying your BW by the current percent fat (%F) expressed in decimal form (e.g., weight of 150, 25% FW: 150 × 0.25 = 37.5)

   FW = BW × %F = _____.

2. Determine lean body mass (LBM) by subtracting the weight in fat from the total BW (e.g., 150 – 37.5 = 112.5).

   LBM = BW – FW = _____.

3. Do this step if you are not in your desired fat percentage range. *If you are in your "desired" fat percentage range, you do not need to calculate your recommended body weight (RBW) using this* formula. Your RBW is computed based on the selected %bf for your age and gender.

   Your decision to select a *desired* fat percentage should be based on your current %bf and your personal health/fitness objectives. Either use the %bf calculated with the bioelectrical impedance device or the girth measurements.

   Select a desired body fat percentage (DFP) based on the health or high fitness standards given in Figure 7-9 on page 254 in your text.

   DFP= _____.

   Compute RBW according to the formula RBW = LBM ÷ (1.0 – DFP).

   RBW = _____.

Discussion

1. According to the results of the measurements you completed, what did you find out about your overall body composition?

2. What do the results tell you about your health? What do you need to change or maintain in order to stay healthy?

Source: Health and Physical Education Program at Western Carolina University. Reprinted with permission.

Resources for Your Personal Health and Wellness

● **Counseling and Psychological Services**
The staff of Counseling Services is trained to address a wide range of presenting concerns and consist of licensed mental health professionals. They are available Monday to Friday, 8 a.m. to 5 p.m., second floor of the Bird Building. To make an appointment, call 227-7469. Their services are FREE and confidential.

● **Student Health Services**
Located in the Bird Building, Student Health Services offers physicals, laboratory tests, sexually transmitted infection (STI) screening, nutrition education, contraceptive options, allergy clinic/immunizations, ambulance service, and doctor's appointments. Your student health fee covers the services provided by the University Health Services. **Some services may have additional fees. Hours of operation are Monday to Friday, 8 a.m. to 5 p.m. To make an appointment, call 227-7640.

● **Campus Recreation Center**
The CRC is located in the heart of campus, right next to Reid Gym. The facilities include cardio and weight equipment, group exercise rooms, a climbing wall, 0.8 indoor track, and gym space. The CRC houses the Recreation and Wellness program that coordinates intramurals, club sports, aquatics (Reid Pool), group exercise classes, personal training, and a wellness programming. The facility is open 7 days a week from early morning to late evening.

● **Base Camp Cullowhee**
Western Carolina University (WCU) is located in an outdoor recreation paradise! Whether you are a seasoned outdoor adventurer or new to the activities, Base Camp Cullowhee (BCC) has programs to help you explore the area. BCC operates the climbing wall in the CRC with open climbing and belay clinics. Some of their programs include kayak roll clinics, skiing and snowboarding at Cataloochee Ski Area, mountain biking, rafting and ducky trips, spring and fall break outdoor adventure trips, fly fishing clinics, hiking, backpacking, and more. They also rent gear.

● **Dining Services**
There are so many options on campus! The hardest thing about being a college student is choosing to eat healthy when there are all you can eat options, such as pizza, burgers, and dessert bars. You can eat healthy in college, just be conscious of your choices. WCU Dining Services provides a website with current menus, nutritional information, and hours of operation.

● **Environmental Wellness in the Whee?**
Do you like to get dirty and eat fresh food? WCU has a Campus Kitchen Garden located behind the WCU baseball field.
Want to reduce your carbon footprint? WCU's Energy Management program can assist you.
What about recycling on campus? Yes, we have that for mixed paper, glass, plastic 1 and 2, and aluminum. Bins are located throughout campus.
Do you really need to drive around looking for a parking space or let her car idle in a parking lot while you wait for someone to leave? No. Parking is available throughout campus, sometimes it is a little bit of a walk to get to your class, but think of it as part of your fitness program and the fact you are saving gas. Bring an umbrella and good walking shoes. Plan ahead and arrive early to campus.

● **Spiritual Wellness in the Whee?**
There is a welcoming community in Cullowhee where you can express your beliefs through traditional worship, academic course work, or campus activities. For information on faith-based organizations and places of worship, and for opportunities to volunteer and give back to the community, contact the office of Service Learning.

- **Making Connections and Getting Involved**

  So you are new to Cullowhee, how do you meet people? In your classes, at events, take a group exercise class, join a club, attend a program in your residence hall, go to an athletic event, and so on.

- **Red Zone Campaign**

  WCU supports its campus community members in their right to healthy, happy, consensual relationships and is dedicated to developing a culture of respect and nonviolence. Early in the first and second year at college, students enter the *Red Zone*, where they are more at risk for unwanted sexual experiences on college campuses. And, according to NCHA 2010 data, 16.5% of WCU men and women report being in an emotionally, physically, or sexually abusive relationship in the past 12 months. As a result, the Red Zone Campaign encourages and empowers students, faculty, and staff to develop an open dialogue on the dangers of sexual violence and to speak up when they see violent behavior occurring. If you notice red flags in yours or a friend's relationship, are experiencing violence or have in the past, you have a number of resources available to you:

  - Counseling and Psychological Services (828-227-7469 or counselingcenter.wcu.edu)

  - REACH of Macon County services in Jackson County (828-586-8969 or www.reachofmaconcounty.org)

For more information, please visit redzone.wcu.edu or contact Sarah Carter at sacarter@wcu.edu.

© wavebreakmedia/Shutterstock.com

Introduction

Americans are among the most obese and overweight people of any developed country in the world. Life expectancy for Americans ranks only 31st in the world (World Health Organization [WHO], 2015), and the current generation of American children are the first to have a potentially shorter life span than their parents. Despite these troubling statistics, our society continues to move toward a more sedentary lifestyle. Perhaps, there has never been a more important time to understand and practice regular physical activity and physical fitness.

Regular exercise will maintain the health of your heart and lungs as well as burn off excess calories to help keep your weight under control. Exercise can also help improve muscle strength, increase joint flexibility, and improve endurance. Another benefit of regular exercise is that it decreases the risk of heart disease, the leading cause of death in America. It can also decrease diabetes, colon cancer, stroke, and high blood pressure. Exercise can also decrease symptoms of anxiety, depression, and stress.

Throughout adulthood is one of the most important times to maintain an exercise regimen. This is the ideal time to maintain or reduce weight, build strong bones, and prevent many chronic health problems. Challenge yourself to find activities that you enjoy, and do them several times over the course of each week for the best benefits.

The FITT Principle

Frequency: How *many* days per week did you do an activity?
Intensity: How *hard* did you work during that activity? Did you meet your goal (i.e., were you in your target heart rate zone)?
Time: How *long* did you do the activity? Try to get at least 30 min of physical activity each day.
Type: What *type* of activity did you do? All types of physical activity can be beneficial to wellness.

© popcic/Shutterstock.com

Target heart rate worksheet   Name: _Mark Melton_

Resting heart rate formula (Record in beats per minute [bpm]):

We will use the Karvonen formula, which estimates heart rate reserve (HRR) and then calculates training heart rates using the formula below.

MHR (maximum heart rate) = 220 – age   HRR = MHR – RHR (resting heart rate)
50% TI (training intensity) = (HRR × 0.50) + RHR
60% TI = (HRR × 0.60) + RHR
85% TI = (HRR × 0.85) + RHR

Example: **Joe is 20 years old. His RHR is 60 bpm.**
MHR = 220 – 20= 200 bpmVA
HRR = 200 – 60= 140 bpm
50% TI = (140 × 0.50) + 60 = 130 bpm
60% TI = (140 × 0.60) + 60 = 144 bpm **Joe's moderate-intensity training heart rate zone (50–60%) = 130–144 bpm**
85% TI = (140 × 0.85) + 60 = 179 bpm **Joe's vigorous-intensity training heart rate zone (60–85%)= 144–179 bpm**

Calculate your maximum heart rate and HRR.

RHR in beats per minute	RHR = 76
220 – age = MHR	MHR = 202
MHR – RHR = HRR	HRR = 126

Calculate your heart rate for each of the training intensities.

TI	Formula	Heart Rate (bpm)	10 Sec Count (divide by 6)
50% TI HRR × 0.50= _63_ + RHR = 139	(Heart Rate Reserve ÷ 2) + Resting HR	139 bpm	23.1$\overline{6}$
60% TI HRR × 0.60= _75.6_ + RHR = 151.6	(Heart Rate Reserve × .6) + Resting HR	151.6 bpm	25.2$\overline{6}$
85% TI HRR × 0.85= _107.1_ + RHR = 183.1	(Heart Rate Reserve × .85) + Resting HR	183.1 bpm	30.51$\overline{6}$

Moderate-intensity training heart rate zone (50–60%)
_____151.6_____ (bpm) _____25.2$\overline{6}$_____ (10 sec count)

Vigorous-intensity training heart rate zone (60–85%)
_____183.1_____ (bpm) _____30.51$\overline{6}$_____ (10 sec count)

Source: Health and Physical Education Program at Western Carolina University. Reprinted with permission.

Static Stretching Worksheet

Date:							
Neck muscles							
Triceps							
Biceps							
Forearm flexors							
Forearm Extensors							
Upper back							
Lower back							
Abs							
Glutes							
Quadriceps							
Hamstrings							
Calves (gastroc)							
Calves (soleus)							
Hip abductors							
Hip adductors							
IT band							
Hip flexor							

Western Carolina University HEAL 123 & HEAL 111   Name: _____

Exercise	Date	Set	1	2	3	1	2	3	1	2	3	1	2	3	1	2	3	1	2	3	1	2	3	1	2	3
		Weights																									
		Reps																									
		Weights																									
		Reps																									
		Weights																									
		Reps																									
		Weights																									
		Reps																									
		Weights																									
		Reps																									
		Weights																									
		Reps																									
		Weights																									
		Reps																									
		Weights																									
		Reps																									
		Weights																									
		Reps																									
		Weights																									
		Reps																									
		Weights																									
		Reps																									
		Weights																									
		Reps																									
		Weights																									
		Reps																									
		Weights																									
		Reps																									

No Equipment Dorm Room Workouts

1. 10 push-ups, 25 sit-ups, 25 flutter kicks × 4; then 50 jumping jacks to finish.
   Push-ups can be done on your knees or toes, sit-ups are done with bent knees and hands across your chest, flutter kicks are done lying on your back with hands under bottom for support. Finish the workout with the "wall stretch for chest," "standing cat stretch," and "modified hurdlers stretch."
2. 10, 9, 8, 7, 6, . . .1 of burpees and squats to a chair. (Don't sit, just touch your bottom to the chair and stand back up to full extension.)
   10 burpees, 10 squats, 9 burpees, 9 squats, and so on.
   Finish with "standing quad stretch," "triceps stretch," and "kneeling hip flexor stretch."
3. 10 push-ups, 30 sec plank hold, 30 sec wall sit × 5. Finish with 3 × 1 min of high knees with 15 sec rest between each minute. Perform "cat and camel," "standing quad stretch," and "overhead reach and lateral stretch."
4. With your desk chair, perform four rounds of 20 chair step-ups, 15 triceps dips using the chair, and 20 mountain climbers. Finish with "gluteal stretch," "triceps stretch," and "kneeling hip flexor stretch."

These stretches are just suggestions. Any of the stretches in your text can be performed if you want to try them! Make sure and hold each stretch *gently* for 15–60 sec.

All workouts are designed to be completed in a fairly short amount of time and include cardio, strength, and flexibility. Pictures of stretches can be found in your textbook. Good luck!

© Syda Productions/Shutterstock.com

Reference

World Health Organization (2017). *Global health observatory data.* Retrieved from www.who.int/gho. (Accessed July 12, 2017).

Introduction

Fueling our bodies is a crucial part of achieving good health. A healthy diet is one of the main components of health and wellness, yet most of us care more about what we put in our car's gas tank than what we put in our own bodies! A poor diet contributes to obesity and other chronic diseases such as cardiovascular disease and cancer.

There are six nutrients: carbohydrates, fats, proteins, vitamins, minerals, and water. The human body needs all of these nutrients to be in optimal health. Most foods can be consumed in moderate amounts, but eating a balanced diet is key.

College students face many food choices, and choosing wisely will affect how you feel right now as well as how your body ages. For example, a diet high in fruits and vegetables can lead to a decreased risk of developing chronic illnesses and help with weight maintenance and management (USDA, 2015). Unfortunately, only 1 in 10 Americans actually meet the recommended intake of fruits and vegetables.

The good news is that in America, today we have more food choices than we have ever had. The key is choosing wisely. This chapter will offer some suggestions on making those healthy choices.

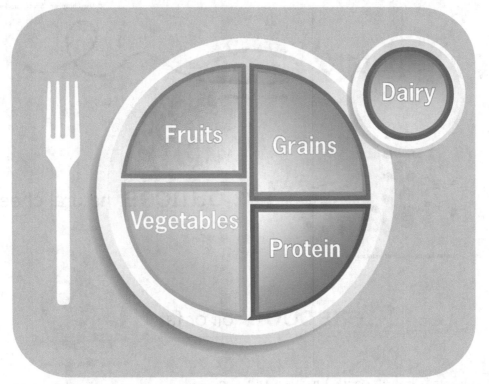

© Basheera Designs/Shutterstock.com

Portion Sizes

1 cup cereal, fruit, vegetables, or cooked rice or pasta

© Ljupco Smokovski/Shutterstock.com

3 ounces meat, fish, or poultry

© Berents/Shutterstock.com

2 tablespoons peanut butter

© Dan Thornberg/Shutterstock.com

1 potato

© sevenke/Shutterstock.com

1½ ounces natural cheese

© Pontus Edenberg/Shutterstock.com

1 teaspoon oil or fat

© testing/Shutterstock.com

Contributed by Aubrey Ray. Copyright © Kendall Hunt Publishing Company.

Dietary Profile Guidelines

© Volkova Anna/Shutterstock.com

The point of this assignment is to help us realize exactly WHAT and HOW MUCH we eat and drink over a 3-day period. Understanding how we eat and what we eat is the first step to making improvements. Lots of times, people underestimate what they are eating and drinking each day.

Each student will keep a record of all food and drink consumed in a 3-day period. Write down *all* the foods/drink that you eat and include how much (your best guess) you eat or drink. For example, if you have a sandwich, that would be two pieces of bread, three slices of turkey, and a piece of cheese. You might also have a tablespoon of mayonnaise (which counts—make sure you don't forget the extras like that in your analysis).

There are a number of good apps for your computer or your phone that can analyze your dietary choices. Choose one that will examine the nutrients in your diet.

Day 1 Food Log (add more rows if you need to)

Date:

When did you eat? *Time of day*	What did you eat? *Type of food or drink*	How much did you eat? *Ingredients and amounts in meal (indicate how it was cooked, e.g., fried, baked)*

Day 2 Food Log (add more rows if you need to)

Date:

When did you eat? *Time of day*	What did you eat? *Type of food or drink*	How much did you eat? *Specific ingredients and amounts in meal (indicate how it was cooked, e.g., fried, baked)*

Day 3 Food Log (add more rows if you need to)

Date:

When did you eat?	What did you eat?	How much did you eat?
Time of day	*Type of food or drink*	*Specific ingredients and amounts in meal (indicate how it was cooked, e.g., fried, baked)*

After all 3 days, please write a paper that addresses the following questions. The paper should be one to two pages typed and should include specific details about each of the questions.

1. How healthy or unhealthy were your foods choices? (Did you get enough of all of the food groups? Did you get a balance of carbs, proteins, and fats?)
2. How healthy or unhealthy were your drink choices? (e.g., Did you drink enough water? Did you consume beverages with a lot of calories?)
3. Discuss the times of day you ate (How often did you eat [how many times during the day]? What times of day did you eat? Did you eat breakfast? Were your meals spread out or concentrated within a short amount of time? Did you see any patterns?)
4. Discuss your portion sizes. Did you have reasonable amounts of all types of food? Did you overload on one particular food?
5. What did you learn about your nutritional habits from keeping the food log? What can you do to improve your nutrition habits?

Grocery Store/Restaurant Discussion Questions

1. Walk around the outer edges of the store. What is different about these aisles compared to the inner aisles?
2. Think about the marketing of products in the supermarket. How are products displayed? Notice where the most expensive products are placed?
3. Now, take a look at the marketing of products to children. List some examples of products that are marketed particularly to kids?
4. Go to the meat section. How is meat labeled? Is the labeling different from other products such as dairy products or other food items?
5. Where is the origin (state or country) of most beef? How about chicken? Does the label tell you where the products came from? What about the seafood? Does it list "Country of Origin"? Where does some of it come from?
6. How do you know if products are grown or farmed locally? Can you find any local products?
7. What about organic products—list some examples. What does *organic* actually mean? Is there a difference in price between organic and nonorganic products?
8. What other *healthy* type labels can you find? Think about terms like *lite*. List the other labels you find. What are the definitions of these terms?
9. Now, wander down the inner aisles. What are some of the products that list high-fructose corn syrup (HFCS) as one of the first or second ingredients?
10. Look in the convenience foods to see if you can find products with palm oil listed. What are some of the products?
11. Read some food labels. Look at the list of ingredients. The order of ingredients is important. Why? Are there ingredients you don't recognize? List an example of a word you don't recognize.
12. Can you find any products that are listed as "genetically modified"? Give some examples.
13. How do we know if our food is safe when we eat out?
14. What does the Health Department score mean? Where is it posted? Is that required?
15. How healthy is the food we eat at restaurants?

Reference

USDA. (2015). *Dietary guidelines for Americans 2015-2020: Dietary guidelines and my plate.* Retrieved from http://www.choosemyplate.gov.

By: Leigh Hilger

Introduction

As a college student, you are building many academic and social skills, and it is important that you build stress management skills too. You may face a variety of stressors during college but with practice you can get better at handling them. Think of your knowledge and skills in stress management as tools to put in your stress management toolbox; the more tools you have, the more options you have for addressing, even preventing, stressors. What kinds of tools are we talking about? Some things you may be doing already, such as getting adequate sleep, recreation, exercise, and social support but others may be new to you, such as deep breathing and other relaxation techniques, time management strategies, and assertive communication skills. These are all positive skills that can go a long way toward lowering stress. In addition to adding positive skills, it is also important to address things you may currently be doing that are actually increasing your stress, such as procrastination and negative thinking.

Get started by working your way through the following pages. You'll assess your current stress level and time management skills, begin planning for better time management and take steps to help you look at your thoughts, anger, and conflict resolution skills. Remember that these new skills will be tools to use now and later to help you keep your stress level down and your happiness level up!

© Makc/Shutterstock.com

How Stressed Are You?

Give yourself one point for every "agree"

1.	I have a hard time falling asleep at night.	Agree	Disagree
2.	I tend to suffer from tension and/or migraine headaches.	Agree	Disagree
3.	I find myself thinking about finances and making ends meet.	Agree	Disagree
4.	I wish I could find more to laugh and smile about each day.	Agree	Disagree
5.	More often than not, I skip breakfast or lunch to get things done.	Agree	Disagree
6.	If I could change my job situation, I would.	Agree	Disagree
7.	I wish I had more personal time for leisure pursuits.	Agree	Disagree
8.	I have lost a good friend or family member recently.	Agree	Disagree
9.	I am unhappy in my relationship or I am recently divorced.	Agree	Disagree
10.	I haven't had a quality vacation in a long time.	Agree	Disagree
11.	I wish my life had a clear meaning and purpose.	Agree	Disagree
12.	I tend to eat more than three meals a week outside the home.	Agree	Disagree
13.	I tend to suffer from chronic pain.	Agree	Disagree
14.	I don't have a strong group of friends to whom I can turn.	Agree	Disagree
15.	I don't exercise regularly (more than three times a week).	Agree	Disagree
16.	I am on prescribed medication for depression.	Agree	Disagree
17.	My sex life is not very satisfying.	Agree	Disagree
18.	My family relationships are less than desirable.	Agree	Disagree
19.	Overall, my self-esteem can be rather low.	Agree	Disagree
20.	I spend no time each day dedicated to meditation or centering.	Agree	Disagree

HOW STRESSED ARE YOU?

Stress Level Key

Less than 5 points	You have a low level of stress and maintain good coping skills
More than 5 points	You a have moderate level of personal stress
More than 10 points	You a have high level of personal stress
More than 15 points	You have an exceptionally high level of stress

© Creativa Images/Shutterstock.com

My Time Management: Time-Crunch Questionnaire

Enter the appropriate points for each question, based on the following guidelines and your current time management skills.

Rarely = 1 point   Sometimes = 2 points   Often = 3 points

1. I tend to procrastinate with projects and responsibilities.   _____
2. My bedtime varies depending on the workload I have each day.   _____
3. I am the kind of person who leaves things till the last minute.   _____
4. I forget to make To-Do lists to keep me organized.   _____
5. I spend more than 2 hr watching television each night.   _____
6. I tend to have several projects going on at the same time.   _____
7. I tend to put work ahead of family and friends.   _____
8. My life is full of endless interruptions and distractions.   _____
9. I tend to spend a lot of time on the phone.   _____
10. Multitasking is my middle name. I am a great multitasker.   _____
11. My biggest problem with time management is prioritization.   _____
12. I am a perfectionist when it comes to getting things done.   _____
13. I never seem to have enough time for my personal life.   _____
14. I tend to set unrealistic goals to accomplish tasks.   _____
15. I reward myself before getting things done in time.   _____
16. I just never have enough hours in the day to get things done.   _____
17. I can spend untold hours distracted while surfing the Internet.   _____
18. I tend not to trust others to get things done when I can do them better myself.   _____
19. If I am completely honest, I tend to be a workaholic.   _____
20. I have been known to skip meals in order to complete projects.   _____
21. I will clean my room, garage, or kitchen before I really get to work on my projects.   _____
22. I will often help friends with their work before doing my own.   _____
23. It's hard to get motivated to get things done.   _____

    TOTAL   _____

Questionnaire Key

75–51 points = Poor time management skills (time to reevaluate your life skills)
50–26 points = Fair time management skills (time to pull in the reins a bit)
0–25 points = Excellent time management skills (keep doing what you are doing!)

Time Tracking

Track how you spend your time. Then, break your time down into categories, such as "sleep," "in class," "studying," "preparing meals/eating," "socializing," and "Internet".

Time period beginning	Number of Hours	Category
7:00 a.m.		
7:30 a.m.		
8:00 a.m.		
8:30 a.m.		
9:00 a.m.		
9:30 a.m.		
10:00 a.m.		
10:30 a.m.		
11:00 a.m.		
11:30 a.m.		
12:00 p.m.		
12:30 p.m.		
1:00 p.m.		
1:30 p.m.		
2:00 p.m.		
2:30 p.m.		
3:00 p.m.		
3:30 p.m.		
4:00 p.m.		
4:30 p.m.		
5:00 p.m.		
5:30 p.m.		
6:00 p.m.		
6:30 p.m.		
7:00 p.m.		
7:30 p.m.		
8:00 p.m.		
8:30 p.m.		
9:00 p.m.		
9:30 p.m.		
10:00 p.m.		
10:30 p.m.		
11:00 p.m.		
11:30 p.m.		
12:00 a.m.		
12:30 a.m.		
1:00 a.m.		
1:30 a.m.		

Time period beginning	Number of Hours	Category
2:00 a.m.		
2:30 a.m.		
3:00 a.m.		
3:30 a.m.		
4:00 a.m.		
4:30 a.m.		
5:00 a.m.		
5:30 a.m.		
6:00 a.m.		
6:30 a.m.		

Total your time: Tally the number of hours spent in each category

Category	No. of hours	Category	No. of hours
		Total no. of hours	24

Contributed by Leigh Hilger. Copyright © Kendall Hunt Publishing Company.

Reflect

1. Is your time being spent in ways that reflect your priorities and values?

2. Is the way you are spending your time adding to or preventing stress?

3. What changes could you make to manage your time more effectively?

Checklist of Cognitive Distortions

1.	**All or nothing thinking**: You look at things in absolute, black and white categories.
2.	**Overgeneralization:** You view a negative event as a never-ending pattern of defeat.
3.	**Mental Filter:** You dwell on the negatives and ignore the positives.
4.	**Discounting the positives:** You insist that your accomplishments or positive qualities "don't count."
5.	**Jumping to conclusions:** (A) Mind reading – you assume that people are reacting negatively to you when there's no definite evidence for this; (B) Fortune Telling – you arbitrarily predict things will turn out badly.
6.	**Magnification or Minimization:** You blow things way out of proportion or you shrink their importance inappropriately.
7.	**Emotional Reasoning:** You reason from how you feel: "I feel like an idiot, so I really must be one." Or "I don't feel like doing this, so I'll put it off."
8.	**"Should Statements":** You criticize yourself or other people with "Shoulds" or "Shouldn'ts." "Musts," "Oughts," "Have tos" are similar offenders.
9.	**Labeling:** You identify with your shortcomings. Instead of saying, "I made a mistake," you tell yourself, "I'm a jerk," or "a fool," or "a loser."
10.	**Personalization and Blame:** You blame yourself for something you weren't entirely responsible for, or you blame other people and overlook ways that your own attitudes and behavior might contribute to a problem.

Adapted from *Feeling Good: The New Mood Therapy* (New York: William Morrow & Company, 1980; Signet, 1981)

Introduction

If you ask a college student how much sleep they've been getting, you might get a smirk or a groan! Why? Because college is typically a time that glorifies late night parties, all night study sessions, and bleary eyes during 8 o'clock classes. But did you know that getting adequate sleep is one of the best things you can do for your body as well as for your grade point average (GPA)? The National Heart, Lung, and Blood Institute states a good night's sleep improves learning. Whether you're learning math, how to play the piano, how to perfect your golf swing, or how to drive a car, sleep helps enhance your learning and problem-solving skills. Sleep also helps you pay attention, make decisions, and be creative.

Studies also show that sleep deficiency alters activity in some parts of the brain. If you're sleep deficient, you may have trouble in making decisions, solving problems, controlling your emotions and behavior, and coping with change. Sleep deficiency also has been linked to depression, suicide, and risk-taking behavior. And, if that isn't reason enough, sleep deficiency has also been linked to heart disease, high blood pressure, diabetes, obesity, and a lowered immune system!

With all of the added pressures of college, please do yourself and your GPA a favor and make sure you get a good night's sleep!

https://www.nhlbi.nih.gov/health/health-topics/topics/sdd/why

© firek1/Shutterstock.com

Chapter 1 Exercise 1.3

Self-Assessment: Poor Sleep Habits Questionnaire

Please take a moment to answer these questions based on your typical behavior. If you feel your sleep quality is compromised, consider that one or more of these factors may contribute to patterns of insomnia by affecting your physiology, circadian rhythms, or emotional thought processing. Although there is no key to determine your degree of insomnia, each question is based on specific factors associated with either a good night's sleep or the lack of it. Use each question to help you fine-tune your "sleep hygiene." Review the material in your text about sleep.

1.	Do you go to bed at about the same time every night?	Yes	No
2.	Does it take you more than thirty minutes to fall asleep once in bed?	Yes	No
3.	Do you wake up at about the same time every day?	Yes	No
4.	Do you drink coffee, tea, or caffeinated soda after 6 p. m.?	Yes	No
5.	Do you watch television from your bed?	Yes	No
6.	Do you perform cardiovascular exercise three to five times per week?	Yes	No
7.	Do you use your bed as your office (e.g., homework, balancing checkbook, Writing letters, etc)?	Yes	No
8.	Do you take hot shower or bath before you go to sleep?	Yes	No
9.	Do you have one or more drinks of alcohol before bedtime?	Yes	No
10.	Are you engaged in intense mental activity before bed (e.g., term papers, exams, projects, reports, finances, taxes?)	Yes	No
11.	Is your bedroom typically warm or even hot before you go to bed?	Yes	No
12.	Does your sleep partner snore or become restless in the night?	Yes	No
13.	Is the size and comfort level of your bed satisfactory?	Yes	No
14.	Do you suffer from chronic pain while lying down?	Yes	No
15.	Is your sleep environment compromised by noise, light, or pets?	Yes	No
16.	Do you frequently take naps during the course of a day?	Yes	No
17.	Do you take medications (e.g. decongestants, steroids, antihypertensive, Asthma, medications or medications for depression)?	Yes	No
18.	Do you tend to suffer from depression?	Yes	No
19.	Do you eat a large, heavy meal right before you go to bed?	Yes	No
20.	Do you use a cell phone regularly, particularly in the evening?	Yes	No

How Much Do You Know About Sleep?

How many hours of uninterrupted sleep did you get last night? What about the night before that? College students are notorious for not getting enough sleep and this sleep deprivation could be making it harder for you to learn and remember information. Take this short quiz to test you sleep knowledge!

1. How many hours of sleep does the average adult need in order to feel fully rested and function at their best?
2. True or False? One night of poor or no sleep does not affect how your brain processes and learns information.
3. True or False? Sleep allows your brain to *clear space* for new learning to occur.
4. True or False? Even if you have had 8 hr of sleep, if you feel *fatigued* you need more sleep.
5. True or False? Chronic sleep deprivation may cause you to gain weight.
6. True or False? Humans are supposed to nap every day.
7. True or False? Having a regular sleep routine is a good way to ensure a good night's rest.
8. True or False? Getting one good night's sleep can reverse the adverse effects of sleep deprivation.
9. True or False? Sleeping in a comfortably warm room is the best way to get a good night's rest.
10. True or False? Constant sensory stimulation (listening to music, looking at your phone or computer) can exhaust the brain as much as sleep deprivation can.

Answers:

1. According to the National Institutes of Health, people 18 yr and older need 7.5–9 hr of sleep per night (Smith, Robinson, & Segal, 2013).
2. False. If you are sleep deprived, you will remember approximately 19% less than normal. If you did not sleep at all, you may remember only 50% of what goes on in class.
3. True. Researchers at University of California (UC) Berkeley have found evidence that while you sleep, electrical impulses in the brain shift memories from the hippocampus to areas with more storage space (Walker, 2005).

4. True. Everyone's sleep needs vary. You may need more than 8 hr.
5. True. Sleep deprivation causes your levels of leptin to drop. Leptin is the hormone that says "I have had enough to eat." Lower leptin levels mean you are hungrier and don't know when to stop!
6. True! Researchers at Stanford University have found that humans naturally become sleepy in the afternoon naturally. You may increase your function and capacity to learn if you take a short nap.
7. True. We are creatures of habit. Having a regular bedtime and wake time helps your body become accustomed to a routine, making it more likely that you are able to fall asleep and wake up refreshed.
8. True. *Recovery* sleep is more efficient than regular sleep, so you can fix a sleep debt with one really great night's sleep.
9. False. Sleeping in a cool (65–68 °F) room allows your body's temperature to naturally dip, enhancing sleepiness.
10. True. Excessive sleepiness and fatigue are two major symptoms of sensory overload.

Sleep, Naps, And Breaks

How many uninterrupted hours of sleep did you get last night? The night before that? When college students are asked about sleep, most report not getting enough. What has your life looked like over the past week? Are you getting as much sleep as you feel you need? We all know that it is more difficult to learn something new when tired, but the role of sleep and fatigue in learning involves more than having difficulty focusing or staying awake when studying. Human sleep is still not fully understood. There is even debate over why we sleep at all. However, most sleep researchers now agree that sleep plays an important role in the formation of long-term memories (Stickgold, 2005).

The exact relationship between memory formation and sleep is the subject of ongoing research, and new evidence is being discovered all the time (see Box 2.1). We do know, however, that the time, money, and effort you put into learning the content and skills in your courses will be significantly diminished by a lack of sleep. Adults typically need 7.5-9 hr of sleep each night to feel fully rested and function at their best. Yet, Americans are getting less sleep than they did in the past. A 2011 National Sleep Foundation (NSF) poll found that about two thirds (63%) of Americans say their sleep needs are not being met during the week. Most say they need about 7.5 hr of sleep to feel their best, but they report getting an average of 6 hr and 55 min of sleep on weeknights. About 15% of adults between 19 and 64 years old and 7% of adolescents between 13 and 18 years old say they sleep less than 6 hr on weeknights (NSF, 2011).

How Neuroscience Findings Change

It was thought for some time that the brain's hippocampus initiated the process that allowed information we wanted to remember to be moved to a more stable area of the brain called the neocortex. Research in 2012 at the University of California-Los Angeles (UCLA) by Mayank Mehta and his colleagues instead showed that the neocortex actually initiates the process. In addition, Mehta found that a part of the brain called the entorhinal cortex plays a significant role in memory formation and involves the hippocampus in memory processing (Mehta, Hahn, McFarland, Berberich, & Sakmann, 2012).

This new finding means that the dialogue among brain areas involved in memory formation is more complex than once thought and that the direction of the communication is the opposite of what was once thought. Memories are still made during sleep, but by a different process.

This example shows that new information about the human brain is discovered all the time, and even the best information we have today may need to be revised as new studies are conducted. All of us as learners will want to pay attention to the new findings.

What Researchers Say

According to the National Institutes of Health, people 18 years old and older need 7.5-9 hr of sleep each night (Smith, Robinson, & Segal, 2013). Mayank Mehta, a neurophysics professor and memory researcher at the University of California-Los Angeles (UCLA), and his colleagues write, "Humans spend one-third of their lives sleeping, and a lack of sleep results in adverse effects on health, as well as learning and memory problems" (Mehta et al., 2012). Neuroscientist Matthew "Walker, director of the Beth Israel Deaconess Medical Center's Sleep and Neuroimaging Laboratory, says, "You can't short-change your brain of sleep and still learn effectively" (as cited in Beth Israel Deaconess Medical Center, 2005). So, if you are not getting 7.5-9 hr of sleep each night, you are likely sabotaging your own learning.

The Science of Memory and Sleep

György Buzsaki, professor at the Center for Molecular and Behavioral Neuroscience at Rutgers University, and his coresearchers have determined that short transient brain events, called sharp wave ripples, are responsible for consolidating memories and transferring new information from the hippocampus, which is a fast-learning but low-capacity short-term memory store, to the neocortex, which is a slower-learning but higher-capacity long-term memory store (Buzsaki, Girardeau, Benchenane, Wiener, & Zugaro, 2009). Information stored in the neocortex will be more stable and have a greater likelihood, if practiced, of becoming long-term memories (see Figure 2.1). Buzsaki et al. (2009) also found that this movement happens primarily when we are asleep.

Dr. James Maas, presidential fellow and past chair of psychology at Cornell University, indicates in *Sleep for Success*, the book he wrote with Rebecca Robbins, that sleep has a big impact on memory (Maas & Robbins, 2011). Maas writes that a person who is sleep deprived will be 19% less efficient at recalling memories. A person who has not slept at all has 50% less memory ability. Maas goes on to write that the final 2 hr of sleep, from hour 5.5 to 7.5 or hour 7 to 9, are crucial for memories to be laid down as stable residents in your brain. During this period in rapid eye movement (REM) sleep, your brain replays scenes from the day over and over again so that they become stable in your memory (Maas & Robbins, 2011).

Sleep helps memory traces to move from the hippocampus to the neocortex, where they are more stable. From www.positscience.com. ©1999 by Scientific Learning Corporation. Reprinted with permission.

Preparation for the Next Day's Learning

Sleep also serves other functions. In addition to providing opportunity to consolidate learned material, sleep allows your brain to clear space for new learning to occur the next day. University of California-Berkeley (UC Berkeley) researchers have found compelling evidence that during sleep 12- to 14-Hz bursts of brain waves, called sleep spindles, may be networking between key regions of the brain to clear a path for learning (Walker, 2005). These electrical impulses help to shift memories from the brain's, hippocampus—which has limited storage space—to the nearly limitless prefrontal cortex's "hard drive," thus freeing up the hippocampus to take in fresh data (new learning).

Matthew Walker says sleep is the key to having a brain that is ready to learn ("Naps Clear the Mind," 2010). Bryce Mander, a postdoctoral fellow in psychology at UC Berkeley and lead author of a study on sleep spindles, adds, "A lot of that spindle-rich sleep is occurring the second half of the night, so if you sleep six hours or less, you are shortchanging yourself and impeding your learning" (as cited in HealthDay News, 2011). Mander goes on to say, "This discovery indicates that we not only need sleep after learning to consolidate what we've memorized, but that we also need it before learning, so that we can recharge and soak up new information the next day" (as cited in HealthDay News, 2011).

Why Sleep Is Crucial to Learning and Memory

Walker says, "When you're asleep, it seems as though you are shifting memories to more efficient storage regions within the brain. Consequently, when you awaken, memory tasks can be performed both more quickly and accurately and with less stress and anxiety" (as cited in Beth Israel Deaconess Medical Center, 2005). Sleep protects new memories from disruption by the interfering experiences that are inevitable during wakefulness (Payne et al., 2012), and during sleep memories are consolidated according to their relative importance, based on your expectations for remembering (Wilhelm et al., 2011). The two key messages here are that, first, new learning is quite fragile and susceptible to change and interference before it is consolidated. REM and slow-wave sleep help to consolidate some memories. Second, according to Payne et al. (2012), "Sleeping soon after learning can benefit both episodic memory (memory for events) and semantic memory (memory for facts about the world)." This means that it would be a good thing to rehearse any information you need to remember immediately before you go to bed. According to Payne et al. (2012), "In some sense, you may be telling' the sleeping brain what to consolidate." As learners, you must identify the new learning you want to remember (Payne et al., 2012).

Three Stages of Memory Processing

The three stages of memory processing are encoding, storage, and retrieval. All three are affected in different ways by the amount of sleep you get. It is difficult to encode new learning when you are tired and unable to pay attention to the information. In fact, when you are sleep deprived, it becomes more difficult to learn new information the longer you are awake. Similarly, without the proper amount of sleep, storage of new memories will be disrupted.

The third stage of memory processing is the recall phase (retrieval). During retrieval, the memory is accessed and re-edited. This is often the most important stage, as learned material is of limited value if it can't be recalled when needed, for example, for an exam. Mass and Robbins (2011) write that recall is impeded by a lack of sleep. Converging scientific evidence, from the molecular to the phenomenological, leaves little doubt that memory reprocessing "offline," that is, during sleep (see Box 2.2) is an important component of how our memories are formed, shaped, and remembered (Stickgold, 2005).

The Stages of Sleep

Non-REM sleep

Stage N1 (Transition to sleep)—This stage lasts about 5 min. Your eyes move slowly under the eyelids, muscle activity slows down, and you are easily awakened.

Stage N2 (Light sleep)—This is the first stage of true sleep, lasting from 10 to 25 min. Your eye movement stops, heart rate slows, and body temperature decreases.

Stage N3 (Deep sleep)—You're difficult to awaken, and if you are awakened, you do not adjust immediately and often feel groggy and disoriented for several minutes. In this deepest stage of sleep, your brain waves are extremely slow. Blood flow is directed away from your brain and toward your muscles, restoring physical energy.

REM sleep

REM sleep (Dream sleep)—About 70 to 90 min after falling asleep, you enter REM sleep, the stage during which dreaming occurs. Your eyes move rapidly, your breathing becomes shallow, and your heart rate and blood pressure increase. Also during this stage, your arm and leg muscles are paralyzed (Smith et al., 2013).

Larks, Night Owls, and the Rest of Us

Humans differ on many dimensions. Sleep is no exception. Individuals do not need the same amount of sleep. In the absence of alcohol, drugs, or sleep challenges, the most important measure of sleep deprivation is simply how you feel. If you are fatigued, then you need more sleep, even if you regularly sleep 8 hr per night. If you feel rested sleeping 6 hr per night, then that is all the sleep you may need. Individuals also differ on the time of day during which they function at an optimal level. For some, early morning is the best time for serious learning, whereas others best learn later at night. Although no large scientific study of adults has been conducted to confirm that people have definite differences in their sleep patterns, many smaller scientific studies suggest that approximately 20–30% of the adult population is made up of either larks (morning people) or night owls (Monk, 2004; Zee & Turek, 2006).

These variations in sleep patterns, or "chronotypes," are a result of our genes, and although they can change as our lives and work schedules change, the process is not often easy to deal with ("Genes Linked," 2011). Dr. Jim Wilson, author of the University of Edinburgh's Centre for Population Health Sciences study of sleep patterns, found that a tendency to sleep for longer or shorter periods often runs in families, although the amount of sleep people need can also be influenced by age, latitude, season, and circadian rhythms ("Genes Linked," 2011).

If you are most alert around noon each day, do your best work in the hours before you eat lunch, and are ready for bed relatively early each night, you are definitively a morning person, or lark. Knowing you are a lark is important information from the standpoint of learning. Larks are much better off taking classes, doing more challenging homework, and studying during the morning or daytime hours and leaving their easier work until night, when they are likely more tired.

If you are most alert around 6:00 p.m., do your best work late in the evening, and often stay up until 2:00 or 3:00 a.m., you are a night owl. Night owls who take morning classes tend to have more difficulty staying awake and paying attention simply because their natural rhythms identify the early morning as a time to sleep. If you are a night owl, sign up for afternoon classes and plan to do challenging homework and study later in the evening.

If you are a night owl, you should avoid attending 8:00 or 9:00 a.m. classes after only 4–6 hr of sleep. In a 2008 study involving more than 800 students, Dr. Kendry Clay of the University of North Texas found that college students who were evening types (night owls) had lower grade point averages (GPAs) than those who were morning types. One reason for this discrepancy was the great likelihood that the night owls were sleep deprived (American Academy of Sleep Medicine, 2008). In a similar 2012 study at the University of Arkansas on the effects, of sleep and anxiety on college students' performance, researchers found that sleep deprivation could lead to a lower GPA (Moran, 2012). Commenting on that study, Kimberly Fenn, the principal investigator at the Sleep and Learning Lab at Michigan State University, said that although occasionally missing an hour of sleep will not be detrimental to academic performance, students who regularly get only 4 or 5 hr of sleep will most likely have a lower GPA (Moran, 2012). For suggestions for changing your night-owl ways, see Box 2.3.

About 70% of the adult population does not fall into either the lark or night-owl category. If you do not have the tendency to get up very early or stay up very late, you simply need to identify your best time of the day for learning.

Most people have not thought carefully about how to structure their day to optimize their learning time according to natural rhythms. One way to do this is to keep a log for one week. Find or make a chart that starts Sunday night at 6:00 p.m. and has blocks for the 24 hr of each day. Each day when you wake up, fill in the blocks to show the time you slept the night before. Then, periodically through the day, give yourself a grade based on how mentally alert you feel. Your grades will vary greatly based on what you are doing, but over time you will likely see patterns. If you read a chapter of a book and feel like you under- stood it well, give yourself an "A," for alert, during that block of reading time. If you are studying and find yourself losing concentration at times, give yourself an "LC," for losing concentration. If you start to do some homework problems and find yourself getting so distracted that you don't accomplish any work, give yourself a "D," for distracted. These are just examples. The idea is to see whether a pattern emerges as to when you concentrate, think, and remember best. You might also see that after a night of almost no sleep, you are "brain dead" most of the next day.

Recommendations for Changing Night-Owl Sleep Patterns

Researchers affiliated with the American Academy of Sleep Medicine suggest that college students reset their internal clocks, a little bit at a time over several weeks, by following these tips:

- Don't pull all-nighters or cram for exams late at night. Instead, do your intense studying in the morning, when your brain is fresh and alert. Schedule study sessions for afternoon.
- Beer and pizza are not good choices close to bedtime. Avoid caffeine, alcohol, heavy exercise, and heavy snacking before bedtime.
- Go to bed at the same time every night—ideally by midnight, so you can get a full night s sleep.
- College kids may consider themselves too old for warm milk and *Goodnight Moon*, but they should make their bedtime routines soothing and consistent. Turn off the cell phone and laptop. Read a book or listen to quiet music.
- Make sure your bedroom is quiet and dark—or if you live in a dorm, invest in a pair of earplugs or noise-cancelling headphones, and a sleep mask.
- Rise at the same time every morning, and get outside. Sunlight helps reset circadian rhythms. (Burrell, 2013)

Naps and Wakeful Rest

Did you know that humans are supposed to nap every afternoon? It's true. Dr. William C. Dement, founder of the Stanford University Sleep Clinic and the father of sleep research, found that the human brain experiences transient sleepiness in the midafternoon and that there is nothing we can do about it. In fact, Dement says humans function best with a good night's rest and a short afternoon nap. A person's desire to nap in midafternoon varies in degree, but the fact remains that our brains do not function well when they want to be asleep (Dement & Vaughan, 1999). Psychologist James Maas points out that naps "greatly strengthen the ability to pay close attention to details and to make critical decisions." He adds that "naps taken about eight hours after you wake have been proven to do much more for you than if you added those 20 or 30 min onto your night time sleep" (Maas & Robbins, 2011, p. 33).

One of the dilemmas we all face is that new memories (information just learned) are stored temporarily in a region of the brain called the hippocampus. "While in this area, newly learned information is fragile and can be easily changed or forgotten. The information needs to be transferred to more permanent storage areas in the brain or else it is susceptible to being replaced by other new learning. Dr. Michaela Dewar and her colleagues, in a study published in *Psychological Science*, found that memory can be boosted by taking a brief wakeful rest after learning something verbally new (Dewar, Alber, Butler, Cowan, &c Della Sala, 2012). The findings of Dewar et al. (2012) suggest that the point at which we experience new information is "just at a very early stage of memory formation and that further neural processes have to occur after this stage for us to be able to remember this information at a later point in time" (p. 35). The authors went on to say that

> researchers believe the new input crowds out recently acquired information, indeed, our work demonstrates that activities that we are engaged in for the first few minutes after learning new information really affect how well we remember this information after a week.

(Dewar et al., 2012) Dewar et al. (2012) demonstrate that activities that we are engaged in for the first few minutes after learning new information affect how well we remember this information. These findings suggest that students should engage in periods of wakeful rest, including daydreaming and thinking, following new learning. The key aspects of this pause are to keep the eyes closed, and to not be distracted or receive new information (Dewar et al., 2012).

The findings of Dewar et al. (2012) suggest, from a learning perspective, that taking classes back-to-back may not be a great idea. Back-to-back class schedules may cut down on travel time to and from campus and allow for better work schedules, but they leave no time for consolidation in the brain of the material presented during the first class.

Another excellent way to consolidate memories, especially if you have afternoon classes, is to take a brief nap of 20-30 min. During this short nap, new learning becomes more stable. Thus, it will more likely be available in its original form when you go to practice it in the future.

Researchers at the University of Lubeck in Germany conducted a study that demonstrated that students who napped after learning 15 pairs of cards with animals on them remembered 85% of the cards, whereas students who learned the same cards but did not nap recalled only 60% (Diekelmann, Büchel, Born, & Rasch, 2011). In another nap study, the National Aeronautics and Space Administration (NASA) found that pilots who took a 26-min nap increased their flying performance by 34% over their performances when no rest was taken. NASA also discovered that a 45-min nap gave astronauts a boost in their cognitive (thinking) performance for 6 hr following the nap (NASA, 2005).

Remembering What Is Important During Sleep

Sleep is important but not equally important for all information. According to a study published in the *Journal of Neuroscience* by Dr. Ines Wilhelm and her colleagues (2011), people remember information better after a good night's sleep when they know it will be useful in the future. This finding suggests that the brain evaluates memories during sleep and preferentially retains those that are most likely to be important and needed relatively soon (Wilhelm et al., 2011). The study also found that the students who slept right after learning new material and who knew they were going to be tested on that material had substantially improved memory recall over students who knew they would not be tested on the newly learned material. The authors suggest that the brain's prefrontal cortex "tags" memories deemed relevant while awake and that the hippocampus consolidates these memories during sleep (Wilhelm et al., 2011).

Sleep Deprivation and Learning

If you are between the ages of 18 and 25, you are part of a generation that seems to love stimulating the brain with multiple and constant sensory inputs. Whether it is listening to music, texting, phoning, watching TV, or playing video games, you are engaging in activities that can exhaust your brain and impede learning, and you may not even be aware that your brain is tired (Berman, Jonides, & Kaplan, 2008). The brain was not built for constant sensory stimulation.

Constantly taxing your brain is not the only way to exhaust it. Another common cause of brain exhaustion is sleep deprivation. One of the most significant findings from sleep researchers is the profound effect getting too little sleep has on learning and memory. A recent University of Cincinnati study showed that only 24% of college students report that they are getting adequate sleep, and a Brown University study showed that only 11% of college students are getting enough sleep (Peek, 2012). Researchers at the University of California—San Francisco discovered that some people have a gene that enables them to do well on 6 hr of sleep a night. But the gene is rare and appears in less than 3% of the population. For the other 97% of us, 6 hr doesn't come close to cutting it (He et al., 2009).

A sleep debt is the difference between the amount of sleep a person should be getting and the amount he or she actually gets. It's a deficit that grows every time we skim some extra minutes off our nightly slumber. Dement and Vaughan (1999) say that people accumulate sleep debt without realizing it and that operating with a sleep debt is bad for learning. The short-term effects of sleep deprivation include a foggy brain, worsened vision, impaired driving, and trouble remembering. Long-term effects include obesity, insulin resistance, and heart disease.

Unfortunately, we are not good at perceiving the detrimental effects of sleep deprivation. Researchers at the University of Pennsylvania restricted volunteers to less than 6 hr in bed per night for two weeks. The volunteers perceived only a small increase in sleepiness and thought they were functioning relatively normally. However, formal testing showed that their cognitive abilities and reaction times progressively declined during the two weeks. By the end of the two-week test, they were as impaired as subjects who had been awake continuously for 48 hr (Van Dongen, Maislin, Mullington, & Dinges, 2003).

In a 2012 study, UCLA professor of psychiatry Andrew J. Fuligni and his colleagues reported that sacrificing sleep for extra study time, whether it's cramming for a test or plowing through a pile of homework, is actually counterproductive. Regardless of how much a student studies each day on average, if that student sacrifices sleep time in order to study more than usual, he or she is likely to have more academic problems, not fewer, the following day ("Cramming," 2012).

Sleeping and Diet

In a 2013 study, Dr. Michael Grandner and his colleagues from the University of Pennsylvania Center for Sleep and Circadian Neurobiology found that people who have a healthy diet and eat a large variety of foods have the healthiest sleep patterns (Lynn, 2013). Numerous studies link sleep deprivation with obesity, so it may not be surprising that a healthy diet is a major predictor of good sleep habits.

Fixing a Sleep Debt

Recovering from one or two night's sleep deprivation is accomplished by getting a good night's rest. Just one night of recovery sleep can reverse the adverse effects of total sleep deprivation. Recovery sleep is more efficient than normal sleep. Most people fall asleep faster than normal and have increased amounts of deep and REM sleep. A good practice is to sleep until you wake up on your own—don't set an alarm.

Recovering from a longer period of sleep deprivation can be trickier. First, you must realize that you are the one who decides how much sleep you get, as you manage the demands on yourself and your time. College allows for many opportunities, but each opportunity comes with a cost of time. For those who have so many obligations that they sleep less than typically recommended and are coping with a long-term sleep debt, the American Academy of Sleep Medicine recommends the following short-term solutions for reducing the effects of sleep deprivation. Note, however, that following these suggestions may not restore alertness and performance to fully rested levels (Widmar, 2003).

- Caffeine: Caffeine is arguably the most commonly ingested stimulant, as it is used regularly by 80% of adults in the United States in liquid, tablet, or gum form. It can provide improved alertness and performance at doses of 75 mg to 150 mg after acute sleep loss. Higher doses are required to produce a benefit after a night or more of total sleep loss. A person who uses caffeine frequently can build up a tolerance to the substance, which makes it less and less effective.
- Naps: During a period of sleep loss, a brief nap of 30 min or less may boost alertness. Be cautious of longer naps, however, because they can be difficult to wake up from and they may also produce severe grogginess, or "sleep inertia," that persists after waking up.
- Caffeine and a nap: The beneficial effects of a nap taken when experiencing sleep deprivation combined with the use of caffeine following the nap may be additive. Combining a nap with caffeine use during sleep deprivation can provide improved alertness over a longer period.
- A doctor visit: Talk to your doctor about why you are failing to get adequate sleep and ask for recommendations for coping with the sleep debt.

Staying Out of Sleep Debt

The following are some additional tips for getting and staying out of sleep debt (Smith et al., 2013):

- Schedule time for sleep and aim for at least 7.5 hr of sleep every night. Block off enough time for sleep each night so that you don't fall further in debt. Consistency is the key.
- Settle short-term sleep debt as soon as possible. Recovery sleep can get you back to optimum learning levels.
- Keep a sleep diary. Record when you go to bed, when you get up, your total hours of sleep, and how you feel during the day. As you keep track of your sleep, you'll discover your natural patterns and get to know your sleep needs.

How to Avoid a Sleep Debt

To avoid falling into a sleep-debt situation, it is important to know how to get a good night's rest. It sounds silly to offer advice on how to do something that is a natural process for all humans, and yet numerous studies indicate that most students don't get enough sleep and that the sleep they do get is not as restful as it needs to be. Following are a few ways to get the quality sleep you need (Smith et al., 2013):

- Pay attention to what you eat and drink. Dont go to bed either hungry or stuffed. Your discomfort might keep you up.
- Be careful when using nicotine, caffeine, and alcohol. The stimulating effects of nicotine and caffeine, which take hours to wear off, can wreak havoc on quality sleep. And even though alcohol might make you feel sleepy, it actually disrupts sleep later in the night.
- Create a bedtime ritual. Do the same things each night to tell your body it's time to wind down. This might include taking a warm bath or shower, reading a book, or listening to soothing music with the lights dimmed.
- Get comfortable. Create a room that's ideal for sleeping. Often this means cool, dark, and quiet.
- Limit daytime naps. Long daytime naps can interfere with nighttime sleep especially if you're struggling with insomnia or poor sleep quality at night. Naps can be very positive but should be limited to one nap of 10–30 min, ideally taken during the midafternoon.

- Include physical activity in your daily routine. Regular physical activity can promote better sleep, helping you to fall asleep faster and to enjoy deeper sleep. However, if you exercise too close to bedtime, you might be too energized to fell asleep.

- Stick to a sleep schedule: Go to bed at the same time every day, even on weekends, holidays, and days off. Being consistent reinforces your body's sleep-wake cycle. There's a caveat, though. If you don't fall asleep within about 15 min, get up and do something relaxing. Go back to bed when you're tired.

- Manage stress. If you are lying in bed and your mind is racing through all you have to do the next day (a common occurrence when under stress), your sleep is likely to suffer. To help restore peace to your life, consider healthy ways to manage stress. Start with the basics, such as getting organized, setting priorities, and delegating tasks. Give yourself permission to take a break when you need one.

- Know when to contact your doctor. Nearly everyone has an occasional sleepless night, but if you frequently have trouble sleeping, or if you are very concerned about your lack of sleep, contact your doctor.

- Listen to Marconi Unions song "Weightless." In the 2011 invention issue of *Time* magazine, the song "Weightless," which lasts 8 min and 10 *s*, was listed as a breakthrough in helping people fall asleep. A listener's body rhythms will sync with the song, slowing heart rate by 35% and reducing anxiety by 65%. Scientists believe that this song works so well that they actually recommend not listening to it while driving.

My Sleep Hygiene and Journal

1. I will go to bed at _____ each night.

2. I will get up at _____ each morning.

3. I will not drink any caffeinated beverages past _____ O'clock.

4. I will get off of my phone/computer _____ minutes before bedtime.

5. I will make sure the room is conducive to sleep by doing the following:

6. I will also do the following to allow my body to prepare for sleep.
   (Example: brush teeth, stretch, perform relaxation exercises, read, etc...)

Date	Time in bed	Time awake	Total hours	Rating of sleep (1–5)

Reflection

1. How strictly did you follow your hygiene plan?

2. Was this a typical week for you? Why or why not?

3. If you followed your plan, did you find that your sleep improved?

4. What else do you think you can do to improve your quality and quantity of sleep?

5. What have you learned about sleep that you did not know before?

Chapter Summary

Sleep is so vital to the human body and brain that a continued lack of it can lead to severe illnesses. Many people know this is true and would never try-to stay awake for days at a time. What many students do not know is that a full night's sleep every night is vital to learning and memory formation. During sleep humans make memories and the human brain clears away unwanted information so that it will be ready to learn the next day. When you are sleep deprived, you impair your ability to pay attention and learn new information, and your brain has trouble making memories for information that you need to remember, such as your course work. Following are the key ideas from this chapter:

1. Memories are made during sleep.
2. Almost every person needs 7.5–9 hr of sleep each night, and teenagers often need even more.
3. Sleep is when the brain clears the hippocampus of unwanted information so that it is ready to learn new information the next day.

4. Each person has his or her own sleep pattern. Some are morning people, some are night owls, and some fall in between. It is important to find your sleep pattern.

5. The brain remembers best what is most important to you, and recalling the most important information right before bed improves memory formation for that information.

6. A daily 20- to 30-min nap is great for improving learning and memory.

7. Constant sensory stimulation of your brain (e.g., listening to music hour after hour or constantly texting) can exhaust the brain and make learning difficult.

8. Sleep deprivation is harmful to learning and memory.

9. If you have significant sleep problems, get help immediately. Sleep is vital to college success.

References

American Academy of Sleep Medicine. (2008, May 15). Morningness a predictor of better grades in college [News release]. Retrieved from http://www.aasmnet.org/articles.aspx?id=887

Berman, M., Jonides, J., & Kaplan, S. (2008, December). The cognitive benefits of interacting with nature. *Psychological Science, 19,* 1207–1212.

Beth Israel Deaconess Medical Center. (2005, June 29). Study shows how sleep improves memory. *Science Daily.* Retrieved from http://www.sciencedaily.com/releases/2005/06/050629070337.htm

Burrell, J. (2013). College kids, sleep and the GPA connection. *About.com Young Adults.* Retrieved from http://youngadults.about.com/od/healthandsafety/a/Sleep.htm

Buzsaki, G., Girardeau, G., Benchenane, K., Wiener, S., & Zugaro, M. (2009). Selective suppression of hippocampal ripples impairs spatial memory. *Nature Neuroscience, 12,* 1222–1223. doi:10.1038/nn.2384

Cramming for a test? Don't do it, say UCLA researchers. (2012, August 22). *UC Health.* Retrieved from http://health.universityofcalifornia.edu/2012/08/22/cramming-for-a-test-don't-do-it-say-ucla-researchers/

Dement, W. C., & Vaughan, H. C. (1999). *The promise of sleep.* New York: Delacourt Press.

Dewar, M., Alber, J., Butler, C., Cowan, N., & Della Sala, S. (2012, September). Brief wakeful resting boosts new memories over the long term. *Psychological Science, 23*(9), 955–960. doi:10.1177/0956797612441220

Diekelmann, S., Biichel, C., Born, J., & Rasch, B. (2011, January 23). Labile or stable: Opposing consequences for memory when reactivated during wakefulness and sleep. *Nature Neuroscience.* doi:10.1038/nn.2744

Genes linked to need for sleep. (2011). *TheFamilyGP.com.* Retrieved from http://www.thefamilygp.com/Genes-linked-to-needing-more-sleep.htm

He, Y., Jones, C. R., Fujiki, N., Xu, Y., Guo, B., Holder, J., . . . Fu, Y. (2009, August). The transcriptional repressor DEC2 regulates sleep length in mammals. *Science, 325*(5942), 866–870. doi:10.1126/science.1174443

HealthDay News. (2011, March 8). *Brain's learning ability seems to recharge during light slumber.* Retrieved from http://www.alegentcreighton.com/body.cfm?id=4794&action=detail&ref=50872

Lynn, J. (2013, February 8). New Penn study links eating, sleeping habits. *Newsworks,* Retrieved from http://www.newsworks.org/index.php/local//healthscience/50754

Maas, J., & Robbins, R. (2011). *Sleep for success.* Bloomington, IN: Authorhouse.

Mehta, M., Hahn, T., McFarland, J., Berberich, S., & Sakmann, B. (2012). Spontaneous persistent activity in entorhinal cortex modulates cortico-hippocampal interaction in vivo. *Nature Neuroscience, 15,* 1531–1538. doi:10.1038/nn.3236

Monk, T. (2004, May). Morningness-eveningness and lifestyle regularity. *Chronobiology International, 21*(3), 435–443.

Moran, D. (2012, September 18). Study shows relationship between sleep and GPA. *State News*. Retrieved from http://statenews.com/index.php/article/2012/09/study_shows_relationship_between_sleep_and_gpa

Naps clear the mind, help you learn. (2010, February 21). *Live Science*. Retrieved from http://www.livescience.com/9819-naps-clear-mind-learn.html

National Aeronautics and Space Administration (NASA). (2005, June 3). *NASA nap study*, http://science.nasa.gov/science-news/science-at-nasa/2005/03jun_naps/

National Sleep Foundation (NSF). (2011, March 7). *Annual sleep in America poll exploring connections with communications technology use and sleep*. Retrieved from http://www.sleepfoundation.org/article/press-release/annual-sleep-america-poll-exploring-connections-communications-technology-use

Payne, J. D., Tucker, M. A., Ellenbogen, J. M., Wamsley, E. J., Walker, M. P., Schacter, D, L., & Stickgold, R. (2012). Memory for semantically related and unrelated declarative information: The benefit of sleep, the cost of wake. *PLoS ONE, 7*(3), e33079. doi:10.1371/journal.pone.0033079

Peek, H. (2012, October 25). Abnormal sleep patterns lead to greater issues. *Tulane Hullabaloo*. Retrieved from http://www.thehullabaloo.com/views/article_2825a6ac-lee4-11e2-ad21-001a4bcf6878.html

Smith, M., Robinson, L., & Segal, R (2013, January). How much sleep do you need? Sleep cycles & stages, lack of sleep, and how to get the hours you need. *HelpGuide.org*. Retrieved from http://www.help-guide.org/life/sleeping.htm

Stickgold, R. (2005, October 27). Sleep-dependent memory consolidation. *Nature, 437*, 1272–1278. doi:10.1038/nature04286

Van Dongen, H., Maislin, G., Mullington, J., & Dinges, D. (2003). The cumulative cost of additional wakefulness: Dose-response effects on neurobehavioral functions and sleep physiology from chronic sleep restriction and total sleep deprivation. *Sleep, 26(2)*, 117–126. Retrieved from http://www.med.upenn.edu/uep/user_documents/dfdl6.pdf

Walker, M. (2005). A refined model of sleep and the time course of memory formation. *Behavioral and Brain Science, 28*, 51–104.

Widmar, R (2003, June 1). Sleep to survive: How to manage sleep deprivation. *Fire Engineering*. Retrieved from http://www.fireengineering.com/articles/print/volume-156/issue-6/features/sleep-to-survive-how-to-manage-sleep-deprivation.html

Wilhelm, I., Diekelmann, S., Molzow, I., Ayoub, A., Molle, M., & Born, J. (2011). Sleep selectively enhances memory expected to be of future relevance. *Neuroscience, 31(5)*, 1563. doi:10.1523/JNEUROSCI.3575-10

Zee, P., & Turek, F. (2006, September). Sleep and health: Everywhere and in both directions. *Journal Archives of Internal Medicine, 166*, 1686–1688.

References

Malinda Smith, Lawrence Robinson, & Robert Segal, (2013). Retrieved from https://www.helpguide.org/.

Walker, Matthew P. (2005). A refined model of sleep and the time course of memory formation. *Behavioral and Brain Sciences, 28*, 51–104.

CHAPTER SIX
CHRONIC DISEASES

By: Chelsea Burrell

Introduction

This chapter will look at chronic diseases and conditions such as heart disease, type 2 diabetes, stroke, cancer, obesity, and arthritis. About half of all adults have one or more chronic health conditions; one of four adults has two or more (Ward, Schiller, & Goodman, 2012). Chronic diseases have steadily increased across several decades, which indicate that many of the risk factors are related to the American lifestyle. According to the Centers for Disease Control and Prevention (CDC), 7 of the top 10 causes of death are chronic diseases. Furthermore, two of these chronic diseases—heart disease and cancer—account for nearly 48% of all deaths (CDC, 2013).

Do you know of someone in your life who suffered or currently suffers from heart disease or cancer? With over 80 million Americans being diagnosed with a form of cardiovascular disease (CVD), odds are that we all know of someone with heart disease or cancer. Knowing someone makes the topic of chronic diseases more personal—it is pertinent that we review information and strategies that could potentially impact our lives now and in the future. For that purpose, this chapter will review CVD and cancer, specifically, and touch on other chronic diseases such as diabetes and arthritis.

In the next few pages, we will discuss family history charts and genetic testing; CVD prevention strategies as well as diagnosis and treatment options; types of cancer as well as prevention strategies, specifically links to physical activity/exercise and cancer, early screening options, symptoms, diagnosis, and treatment; type 2 diabetes information; and brief arthritis prevention and treatment options.

© shahreen/Shutterstock.com

CVDs

CVDs	CVD definitions
1. Coronary artery disease	1. Disease of the arteries of the heart → buildup of fats and reduction of blood flow
2. Stroke	2. Interruption of blood and oxygen to parts of the brain
3. Peripheral artery disease	3. Damage or dysfunction of arteries in the limbs
4. High blood pressure (hypertension)	4. Sustained high blood pressure (BP)
5. Heart failure	5. Unable to pump blood at a sufficient rate
Cardiovascular risk factors	**CVD prevention**
1. Genetic history	1. Choose a healthy diet and activity level
2. 70% increased risk over the age of 60	2. Avoid tobacco
3. Men are more likely to develop CVD	3. Moderate alcohol use
4. African Americans are at higher risk for hypertension	4. Manage stress
5. American Indians are at a higher risk for stroke	5. Have regular screenings
Healthy diet tips to avoid CVD/CVD treatment	**Treatment options**
• More fiber, fruits, vegetables, legumes, low-fat dairy products, and fish	• Coronary angioplasty
• Grilled, baked, or broiled > fried	• Coronary bypass
• Whole wheat and grains > white grain	• Pacemaker
• Olive oil > butter	• Heart valve repair/replacement
• Smaller portions > bigger portions	• Heart transplant

Cancer

Cancer types	Risk of cancer
1. Carcinoma • Breast, lung, bladder, colon, ovarian, skin, etc.	• Genetic and family history
2. Sarcoma • Bone, cartilage, fat, muscle, blood vessels, and tendons	• 77% increase in ages 55 or older
3. Lymphoma and myeloma • Immune system	• Half of men and one third of women get cancer
4. Leukemia • Bone marrow	• African Americans have highest rate of cancer
5. Central nervous system • Brain or spinal cord	• Exposure to cancer-causing agents
Symptoms of cancer	**Prevention of cancer**
C—Changes in bowl or bladder habits	• Genetic testing
A—A sore that does not heal	• Regular checkups and early screenings
U—Unusual bleeding or discharge	• Avoid tobacco
T—Thickening or lump in the breast or elsewhere	• Healthy diet and exercise
I—Indigestion or difficulty swallowing	• Maintain a healthy body weight
O—Obvious changes in wart or mole	• Limit alcohol intake
N—Nagging cough or hoarseness	• Minimize infectious agents
	• Radiation
	• Limit sunlight and tanning lamps
	• Avoid high stress
	• Avoid chemicals

American Institute for Cancer Research suggestions to reduce risk

Food to fight cancer:
- Apples, blueberries, broccoli, carrots, cranberries, dark green leafy vegetables, dry beans and peas, flaxseed, garlic, grapefruit, grapes and grape juice, soy, squash (winter), tea (herbal), tomatoes, walnuts, and whole grains.

© girafchik/Shutterstock.com

Diabetes and Arthritis

Diabetes

Type 1: Little or no insulin secretion due to an autoimmune disease that destroys the insulin-producing cells

Type 2: Impaired insulin use by the cells and, in some cases, insufficient insulin production
- Most common form

Risk factors for diabetes
- Over the age of 45
- Body mass index (BMI) over 25
- Inactive
- Family history
- High BP or cholesterol
- Blood glucose levels that are higher than normal
- Blood vessel problems affecting the heart, brain, or legs
- Dark, thick, velvety skin around the neck or in the armpits
- Polycystic ovary syndrome

Diagnosis and treatment of diabetes

Diagnosis
- A1C test
- Fasting plasma glucose test
- Oral glucose tolerance test

Treatment

Type 1: daily insulin shots or insulin pump

Type 2: oral medications and lifestyle changes

Prevention strategies for diabetes
- Regular physical activity
- Low-fat and low-calorie diet
- Maintain healthy BP and cholesterol levels

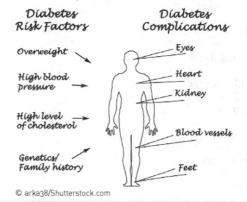

© arka38/Shutterstock.com

Arthritis

Osteoarthritis: Joint pain and progressive stiffness that develops gradually.

Rheumatoid arthritis: Painful swelling, inflammation, and stiffness in the fingers, arms, legs, and wrists.

Arthritis treatment

Treatment can help, but this condition cannot be cured. It requires a medical diagnosis—lab tests and imaging are often required.
- Medications
- Physical therapy

Family History Form

Medical condition	Mom	Dad	Sister	Brother	Mom's mom	Mom's dad	Dad's dad	Dad's mom
Family history: Please indicate relatives with these conditions								
Anemia								
Asthma								
Autoimmune disorder								
Bleeding problems								
Breast cancer								
Melanoma								
Ovarian cancer								
Congenital anomaly								
Heart disease/ heart attack								
Depression								
Diabetes								
Food allergy								
Genetic Disorder								
Hypertension								
Immune disorder								
Kidney disease								
Stroke								
Substance abuse								
Thyroid disorder								
Tobacco use								
Lung cancer								
Prostate cancer								
Arthritis								
Other								

Early Screening

Be sure to have regular checkups with your local doctor—medical exams can help with early detection.

- Screening tests
  - ✓ Mammogram
  - ✓ Colonoscopy
  - ✓ Cholesterol measurements
  - ✓ Fecal blood test
  - ✓ Pap test
  - ✓ Prostate-specific antigen
- Diagnostic tests
- Medical exams
- Self-exams

Contributed by Chelsea Burrell. Copyright © Kendall Hunt Publishing Company.

Sources

American Institute for Cancer Research. (2007). *Food, nutrition, physical activity and the prevention of cancer: A global perspective*. Retrieved from http://www.aicr.org/reduce-your-cancer-risk/smoking-and-other-lifestyle-factors/preventing-half-of-cancer.html

American Institute for Cancer Research. (2007). *Recommendations for cancer prevention*. Retrieved from http://www.aicr.org/reduce-your-cancer-risk/recommendations-for-cancer-prevention/

American Institute for Cancer Research. (2009). *Policy and action for cancer prevention*. Retrieved from http://www.aicr.org/reduce-your-cancer-risk/smoking-and-other-lifestyle-factors/preventing-half-of-cancer.html

American Institute for Cancer Research. (2017). *Physical activity and lower cancer risk*. [Infographic]. Retrieved from http://www.aicr.org/learn-more-about-cancer/infographics/infographic-being-physically-active-decreases-risk-of-these-cancers.html

Centers for Disease Control and Prevention (CDC). (2013, December). *Death and mortality*. NCHS FastStats. Retrieved from http://www.cdc.gov/nchs/fastats/deaths.htm

Diabetes 101. (2017). *Diabetes 101: Herbal and natural remedies for diabetes*. Retrieved from http://thecornerinthemiddle.com/type-2-diabetes/

Levy, D. Cancer Prevention Through a Healthy Diet & Lifestyle. (2014, October). Retrieved from http://daniellelevynutrition.com/2014/10/19/cancer-prevention-through-a-healthy-diet-lifestyle/

Liguori, G., & Sandra, C.-C. (2016). *Questions and answers a guide to fitness and wellness*. New York, NY: McGraw Hill Education.

Pediatric Family History Form. (2008, September). *Palo alto medical foundation*. Retrieved from http://www.efoza.com/postpic/2010/05/family-medical-history-forms-templates_484766.png

U.S. Department of Health and Human Services, National Institute of Diabetes and Digestive and Kidney Diseases. (2012). Diabetes Prevention Program. Retrieved from https://www.niddk.nih.gov/about-niddk/research-areas/diabetes/diabetes-prevention-program-dpp/Pages/default.aspx

Ward, B. W., Schiller. J. S., & Goodman, R. A. (2014). Multiple chronic conditions among US adults: A 2012 update. *Preventing Chronic Disease, 11*, 130389. doi:10.5888/pcd11.1303 89*Contributed by Chelsea Burrell. Copyright © Kendall Hunt Publishing Company.*

CHAPTER SEVEN

SEXUALITY, GENDER, AND RELATIONSHIPS

By: Aubrey Ray

© RyFlip/Shutterstock.com

Introduction

Relationships that are physically and emotionally healthy are crucial to maintaining overall wellness. This may include relationships with friends, family, romantic and sexual partners, coworkers, classmates, roommates, and others. Maintaining these relationships requires an understanding of your identity, values, and expectations in relationships. It also requires skills to effectively communicate, solve problems, and show support for one another.

In sexual relationships, skills for avoiding sexual violence and preventing unintended pregnancies and transmission of sexually transmitted infections (STIs) are also important. Half of all sexually active people will contract an STI at some point in their lifetime. Many of those will contract an STI before the age of 25. Additionally, one in six women in the United States will experience an attempted or completed rape. When looking at all types of sexual violence, the rate rises to one in four. College students are a high-risk group for sexual assault. The first 6 weeks of the fall semester each year is often referred to as the "Red Zone," because it is the time that sexual assaults are most likely to occur. Being in a new environment, meeting new people, and experimenting with alcohol and other drugs contribute to the high rates of sexual assault during that time.

Understanding your own identity and effectively communicating with others to build safe, healthy relationships can be challenging but it is essential to living a happy, healthy life. In this section, you will find information, assessments, and resources to help you examine and strengthen your relationship skills.

Healthy Relationship Quiz

Answer yes or no to each of the following questions.

1. Can you name at least five characteristics of your partner that you admire?
2. Does your partner regularly express the characteristics they admire about you?
3. Is your partner glad that you have other friends?
4. Are you glad that your partner has other friends?
5. Does your partner ask for your opinion on things?
6. Do you ask your partner for their opinion on things?
7. Does your partner do thoughtful things for you?
8. Do you do thoughtful things for your partner?
9. Does your partner express appreciation for the things you do for them?
10. Do you express appreciation for the things your partner does for you?
11. Does your partner get pleasure from doing things that you enjoy?
12. Do you get pleasure from doing things that your partner enjoys?
13. Does your partner have good relationships with *their* family and friends? With *your* family and friends?
14. Do you have good relationships with *your* family and friends? *Your partner's* family and friends?
15. Does your partner both talk and listen?
16. Do you both talk and listen?
17. Do you consider your partner a friend?
18. Does your partner consider you a friend?
19. Do you feel and act "like yourself" when you are with your partner?
20. Does your partner feel and act like their self when they are with you?
21. Does your partner have their own interests and hobbies outside the relationship?
22. Do you have your own interests and hobbies outside the relationship?
23. Do you and your partner have similar values?
24. Do you and your partner contribute equally to the relationship?
25. Does your partner constantly ask where you have been, who you have been with, and so on, when you are away from each other?
26. Do you constantly ask your partner where they have been, who they have been with, and so on, when you are away from each other?

27. Does your partner constantly call or text when you are away from each other?
28. Do you constantly call or text your partner when you are away from each other?
29. Does your partner lose their temper easily?
30. Do you lose your tempter easily?
31. Is your partner jealous of your friends, ex-partners, or family members?
32. Are you jealous of your partner's friends, ex-partners, or family members?
33. Does your partner get upset when they are not the focus of your attention?
34. Do you get upset when you are not the focus of your partner's attention?
35. Does your partner require you to do most of the work in the relationship?
36. Do you require your partner to do most of the work in the relationship?
37. Does your partner dismiss, ignore, or invalidate your feelings?
38. Do you dismiss, ignore, or invalidate your partner's feelings?
39. Does your partner refuse to take responsibility for their actions/mistakes?
40. Do you refuse to take responsibility for your actions/mistakes?
41. Does your partner ignore you or mistreat you when they are upset?
42. Do you ignore or mistreat your partner when you are upset?
43. Does your partner act secretive or lie about things?
44. Do you act secretive or lie about things?
45. Does your partner ever throw, hit, or break things when they are angry?
46. Do you ever throw, hit, or break things when you are angry?
47. Does your partner use alcohol in excess or use other drugs?
48. Do you use alcohol in excess or use other drugs?

Answering yes to most or all of questions 1–24, may be considered a foundation for a healthy relationship. Notice, most of these questions require you to reflect on your partner's behavior and your own behavior. In order for a relationship to be healthy, both partners must engage in behaviors that build and strengthen the relationship.

Answering yes to any of questions 25–48 may be an indicator of an unhealthy relationship. Notice those questions also require you to reflect on your partner's behavior and your own behavior. If either partner engages in an unhealthy relationship behavior, it can be harmful to the relationship.

If you were unable to answer yes to some of the questions on the first half of the list or answered yes to any questions on the second half of the list, consider talking to your partner and a trusted friend, family member, or professional about those issues. That can help you to determine if those behaviors can be improved or if it would be healthier to end the relationship.

Characteristics of a healthy relationship:

- Both partners feel safe communicating openly and honestly about their feelings and needs
- Conflict is handled respectfully and each partner strives to find a resolution
- Both partners engage in conversation by talking and listening
- Boundaries are clear and explicit but allow flexibility if necessary
- Each partner feels supported and accepted
- Each partner can take care of their self and also enjoys doing things to take care of the other
- Each partner enjoys playing, laughing, and having fun together
- Neither partner tries to "fix" or control the other
- Each partner is able to let go of the need to "be right"
- Each partner is confident in who they are as an individual

Contributed by Aubrey Ray. Copyright © Kendall Hunt Publishing Company.

Can you think of other characteristics of a healthy relationship? Add those here.

- _____
- _____
- _____
- _____
- _____
- _____
- _____
- _____
- _____
- _____

Your Birth Control Choices

Method	How well does it work?	How to Use	Pros	Cons
The Implant Nexplanon®	> 99%	A health care provider places it under the skin of the upper arm It must be removed by a health care provider	Long lasting (up to 4 years) No pill to take daily Often decreases cramps Can be used while breastfeeding You can become pregnant right after it is removed	Can cause irregular bleeding After 1 year, you may have no period at all Does not protect against human immunodeficiency virus (HIV) or other sexually transmitted infections (STIs)
Progestin IUD Liletta®, Mirena®, Skyla® and others	> 99%	Must be placed in uterus by a health care provider Usually removed by a health care provider	May be left in place 3 to 7 years, depending on which IUD you choose No pill to take daily May improve period cramps and bleeding Can be used while breastfeeding You can become pregnant right after it is removed	May cause lighter periods, spotting, or no period at all Rarely, uterus is injured during placement Does not protect against HIV or other STIs

Method	How well does it work?	How to Use	Pros	Cons
Copper IUD ParaGard®	> 99%	Must be placed in uterus by a health care provider Usually removed by a health care provider	May be left in place for up to 12 years No pill to take daily Can be used while breastfeeding You can become pregnant right after it is removed	May cause more cramps and heavier periods May cause spotting between periods Rarely, uterus is injured during placement Does not protect against HIV or other STIs
The Shot Depo-Provera®	94-99%	Get a shot every 3 months	Each shot works for 12 weeks Private Usually decreases periods Helps prevent cancer of the uterus No pill to take daily Can be used while breastfeeding	May cause spotting, no period, weight gain, depression, hair or skin changes, change in sex drive May cause delay in getting pregnant after you stop the shots Side effects may last up to 6 months after you stop the shots Does not protect against HIV or other STIs
The Pill	91-99%	Must take the pill daily	Can make periods more regular and less painful Can improve PMS symptoms Can improve acne Helps prevent cancer of the ovaries You can become pregnant right after stopping the pills	May cause nausea, weight gain, headaches, change in sex drive - some of these can be relieved by changing to a new brand May cause spotting the first 1-2 months Does not protect against HIV or other STIs

(Continued)

(Continued)

Method	How well does it work?	How to Use	Pros	Cons
Progestin-Only Pills	91-99%	Must take the pill daily	Can be used while breastfeeding You can become pregnant right after stopping the pills	Often causes spotting, which may last for many months May cause depression, hair or skin changes, change in sex drive Does not protect against HIV or other STIs
The Patch Ortho Evra®	91-99%	Apply a new patch once a week for three weeks No patch in week 4	Can make periods more regular and less painful No pill to take daily You can become pregnant right after stopping patch	Can irritate skin under the patch May cause spotting the first 1-2 months Does not protect against HIV or other STIs
The Ring Nuvaring®	91-99%	Insert a small ring into the vagina Change ring each month	One size fits all Private Does not require spermicide Can make periods more regular and less painful No pill to take daily You can become pregnant right after stopping the ring	Can increase vaginal discharge May cause spotting the first 1-2 months of use Does not protect against HIV or other STIs
Male/External Condom	82-98%	Use a new condom each time you have sex Use a polyurethane condom if allergic to latex	Can buy at many stores Can put on as part of sex play/foreplay Can help prevent early ejaculation Can be used for oral, vaginal, and anal sex Protects against HIV and other STIs Can be used while breastfeeding	Can decrease sensation Can cause loss of erection Can break or slip off

Method	How well does it work?	How to Use	Pros	Cons
Female/Internal Condom	79-95%	Use a new condom each time you have sex Use extra lubrication as needed	Can buy at many stores Can put in as part of sex play/foreplay Can be used for anal and vaginal sex May increase pleasure when used for vaginal sex Good for people with latex allergy Protects against HIV and other STIs Can be used while breastfeeding	Can decrease sensation May be noisy May be hard to insert May slip out of place during sex
Withdrawal Pull-out	78-96%	Pull penis out of vagina before ejaculation (that is, before coming)	Costs nothing Can be used while breastfeeding	Less pleasure for some Does not work if penis is not pulled out in time Does not protect against HIV or other STIs Must interrupt sex
Diaphragm Caya® and Milex®	88-94%	Must be used each time you have sex Must be used with spermicide	Can last several years Costs very little to use May protect against some infections, but **not HIV** Can be used while breastfeeding	Using spermicide may raise the risk of getting HIV Should not be used with vaginal bleeding or infection Raises risk of bladder infection
Fertility Awareness Natural Family Planning	76-95%	Predict fertile days by: taking temperature daily, checking vaginal mucus for changes, and/or keeping a record of your periods It works best if you use more than one of these Avoid sex or use condoms/spermicide during fertile days	Costs little Can be used while breastfeeding Can help with avoiding or trying to become pregnant	Must use another method during fertile days Does not work well if your periods are irregular Many things to remember with this method Does not protect against HIV or other STIs

(Continued)

(Continued)

Method	How well does it work?	How to Use	Pros	Cons
Spermicide Cream, gel, sponge, foam, inserts, film	72-82%	Insert spermicide each time you have sex	Can buy at many stores Can be put in as part of sex play/foreplay Comes in many forms: cream, gel, sponge, foam, inserts, film Can be used while breastfeeding	May raise the risk of getting HIV May irritate vagina, penis Cream, gel, and foam can be messy
Emergency Contraception Pills Progestin EC (Plan B® One-Step and others) and ulipristal acetate EC (ella®)	58-94% Ulipristal acetate EC works better than progestin EC if you are overweight Ulipristal acetate EC works better than progestin EC in the 2-5 days after sex	Works best the **sooner** you take it after unprotected sex You can take EC up to 5 days after unprotected sex If pack contains 2 pills, take both together	Can be used while breastfeeding Available at pharmacies, health centers, or health care providers: call ahead to see if they have it People of any age can get some brands without a prescription	May cause stomach upset or nausea Your next period may come early or late May cause spotting Does not protect against HIV or other STIs If you are under age 17 you may need a prescription for some brands Ulipristal acetate EC requires a prescription May cost a lot

Reprinted by permission of Reproductive Health Access Project.

STI Fact Sheet

STI	Pathogen	Typical cause or method of transmission	Possible symptoms	Test	Treatment
Bacterial vaginosis	Bacteria	Imbalance of normal bacteria and yeast	Strong odor, increased discharge, vaginal discomfort	Genital swab	Cured with antibiotics
Chlamydia	Bacteria	Semen or vaginal fluid	Often asymptomatic, discharge, burning during urination	Urine test or genital/oral/anal swab	Cured with antibiotics
Gonorrhea	Bacteria	Semen or vaginal fluid	Often asymptomatic, discharge, burning during urination, sore throat, anal itching or discharge	Urine test or genital/oral/anal swab	Cured with antibiotics
Hepatitis A	Virus	Contact with fecal matter	Nausea, loss of appetite, fever, jaundice, fatigue, abdominal pain, dark urine	Blood test	Clears from the body, no treatment needed, vaccine prevents the infection
Hepatitis B	Virus	Blood, semen or vaginal fluid	Often asymptomatic, nausea, poor appetite, fever, jaundice, abdominal pain, dark urine	Blood test	Usually managed with medication, virus may stay in the body or clear on its own, vaccine prevents infection
Hepatitis C	Virus	Blood	Often asymptomatic, nausea, poor appetite, fever, jaundice, abdominal pain, dark urine	Blood test	Usually managed with medication, virus may stay in the body or clear on its own
Herpes simplex virus (HSV)	Virus	Sexual skin-to-skin contact, fluid in sores	May not notice symptoms, painful blisters on the genitals, mouth, or face	Visual exam, blood test, or genital/oral/anal swab	Usually managed with medication, virus may stay in the body or clear on its own
Human immunodeficiency virus (HIV)	Virus	Blood, semen or vaginal fluid	May not notice symptoms, flu-like illness, swollen lymph nodes, skin rash	Blood test	Manage symptoms and slow the progression of the disease with medication, virus stays in body

(Continued)

STI	Pathogen	Typical cause or method of transmission	Possible symptoms	Test	Treatment
Human papilloma virus (HPV)	Virus	Sexual skin-to-skin contact	May not notice symptoms, painless bumps around the genitals or buttocks (genital warts)	Visual exam or genital/oral/anal swab	Most infections will clear on their own, genital warts may be treated with medication, vaccine prevents infections from four to nine most dangerous strains
Molluscum contagious	Bacteria	Sexual skin-to-skin contact	Small, firm, painless pink/white bumps on the skin	Visual exam	Virus clears from the body over time, sometimes treated with topical medication
Pubic lice	Parasite	Sexual skin-to-skin contact	Genital itching, visible lice in the pubic hair	Visual exam	Treated with topical medication
Scabies	Parasite	Sexual skin-to-skin contact	Itching and rash	Visual exam	Treated with topical medication
Syphilis	Bacteria	Sexual skin-to-skin contact, semen or vaginal fluid	May not notice symptoms, open sores on the skin followed by a rash	Blood test	Cured with antibiotics
Trichomoniasis	Parasite	Semen or vaginal fluid	Discharge, burning during urination, painful sex	Genital swab	Cured with antibiotics
Yeast/thrush	Fungus	Imbalance of normal bacteria yeast	Genital itching, soreness, and dryness; painful sex; thick white discharge	Genital/oral/anal swab	Cured with topical or oral antifungal medication

Notes:
This list includes most but not all STIs.
Some of the STIs on this list can develop or be transmitted through nonsexual behaviors in addition to the sexual behaviors listed.
Other infections can cause similar symptoms to those on this list.
It is wise to get tested regularly if you are sexually active. If you experience any of these symptoms, or believe you have been exposed to an STI, contact Student Health Services (828-227-7640) or the Jackson County Department of Public Health (828-586-8994) for testing and treatment.

Four Basic Communication Styles

	Passive	Aggressive	Passive-aggressive	Assertive
Goal	To avoid conflict or being judged	To have own opinion heard and accepted by others	To get a point across without directly addressing the issue	To express views, listen to others' views, and seek a solution
Verbal characteristics	Keeps quiet Agrees with others despite personal views Doesn't express own views or apologizes for expressing them	Expresses views as if no other views are valid Ignores or dismisses other views	Uses sarcasm, indirect communication, or "back-handed compliments" Complains about issues but doesn't directly address them	Expresses views in a way that is direct honest, and respectful Listens to others' views Accepts differing views as valid Seeks mutually beneficial solutions
Nonverbal characteristics	Maintains a small or closed off posture Avoids eye contact Maintains more than appropriate distance from others Speaks softly/quietly	Maintains a large posture, uses large gestures Maintains excessive, fixed, or penetrating eye contact Maintains less than appropriate distance from others Speaks loudly, may shout	Usually mimics passive style May exhibit characteristics of aggressive type also	Maintains a relaxed, open posture Uses frequent, appropriate eye contact Maintains a comfortable, appropriate distance from others Speaks using appropriate, moderate voice volume

Reflection questions:

- Which communication style comes more naturally to you?
- Which communication style do you use most often?
- Which communication style is healthiest (most helpful in solving problems and building relationships)?
- Why are the other communication styles less healthy?
- Are there situations in which the "less healthy" communication styles may be appropriate?
- Considering the characteristics of these communication styles, what is one communication skill you would like to work on improving?

Contributed by Aubrey Ray. Copyright © Kendall Hunt Publishing Company.

The Right Way to Use a Male Condom

Condom Dos and Don'ts

- **DO** use a condom every time you have sex.
- **DO** put on a condom before having sex.
- **DO** read the package and check the expiration date.
- **DO** make sure there are no tears or defects.
- **DO** store condoms in a cool, dry place.
- **DO** use latex or polyurethane condoms.
- **DO** use water-based or silicone-based lubricant to prevent breakage.

- **DON'T** store condoms in your wallet as heat and friction can damage them.
- **DON'T** use nonoxynol-9 (a spermicide), as this can cause irritation.
- **DON'T** use oil-based products such as baby oil, lotion, petroleum jelly, or cooking oil because they will cause the condom to break.
- **DON'T** use more than one condom at a time.
- **DON'T** reuse a condom.

How to Put On and Take Off a Male Condom

1. Carefully open and remove condom fromwrapper.

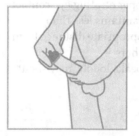

2. Place condom on the head of the erect, hard penis. If uncircumcised, pull back the foreskin first.

3. Pinch air out of the tip of the condom.

4. After sex but before pulling out, hold the condom at the base. Then pull out, while holding the condom in place.

5. After sex but before pulling out, hold the condom at the base. Then pull out, while holding the condom in place.

6. Carefully remove the condom and throw it in the trash.

Content source: National Center for HIV/AIDS, Viral Hepatitis, STD, and TB Prevention, Centers for Disease Control and Prevention.

How to Use a Dental Dam as a Barrier for Oral Sex

Dental dams are latex or polyurethane sheets used between the mouth and vagina or anus during oral sex. Ready-to-use dental dams can be purchased online.

Dental Dam Dos and Don'ts

- **DO** use a new latex or polyurethane dental dam every time you have oral sex.
- **DO** read the package and check the expiration date.
- **DO** make sure there are no tears or defects.
- **DO** put on before starting oral sex and keep it on until finished.
- **DO** use water-based or silicone-based lubricant to prevent breakage.
- **DO** store dental dams in a cool, dry place.

- **DON'T** reuse a dental dam.
- **DON'T** stretch a dental dam, as this can cause it to tear.
- **DON'T** use nonoxynol-9 (a spermicide), which can cause irritation.
- **DON'T** use oil-based products such as baby oil, lotion, petroleum jelly, or cooking oil because they will cause the dental dam to break.
- **DON'T** flush dental dams down the toilet as they may clog it.

How to Use a Dental Dam

 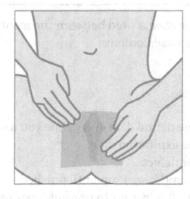 

1. Carefully open dental dam and remove from package.

2. Place dental dam flat to cover vaginal opening or anus.

3. Throw away used dental dam in trash.

How to Make a Dental Dam From a Condom*

1. Carefully open package, remove condom, and unroll.

2. Cut off tip of condom.

3. Cut off bottom of condom.

4. Cut down one side of condom.

5. Lay flat and to cover vaginal opening or anus.

Content Source: National Center for HIV/AIDS, Viral Hepatitis, STD, and TB Prevention; Centers for Disease Control and Prevention.

Be sure the condom is made of latex or polyurethane.

Sexuality and Gender Terminology

Aspects of sexuality and gender:

- **Biological sex**: A classification based on an individual's reproductive organs, hormones, and chromosomes (e.g., female, male, intersex)
- **Gender identity**: A mental and emotional identification of an individual's own gender (e.g., man, woman, genderqueer, gender fluid, bi-gender, agender).
- **Gender expression**: The ways in which people externally communicate their gender identity to others through social cues (e.g., feminine, masculine, androgynous).
- **Sexual identity**: An identification based on who an individual is physically or sexually attracted to (e.g., heterosexual, gay, lesbian, bisexual, pansexual, asexual, demisexual).
- **Sexual behavior**: The types of sexual activity that an individual engages in.
- **Romantic identity**: An identification based on who an individual is romantically attracted to (e.g., heteroromantic, homoromantic, biromantic, panromantic, aromantic).

Sexual identity terms:

- **Heterosexual**: Describes someone who is sexually attracted to people of the opposite sex.
- **Gay**: Describes a man who is sexually attracted to men, or an umbrella term for someone (male or female) who is attracted to people of the same sex.
- **Lesbian**: Describes a woman who is sexually attracted to women.
- **Bisexual**: Describes someone who is sexually attracted to both men and women (or any two genders).
- **Pansexual**: Describes someone who is sexually attracted to people of all or many genders (men, women, cisgender, transgender, genderqueer, etc.).
- **Asexual**: Describes someone who is not sexually attracted to people of any gender.
- **Demisexual**: Describes someone who is only sexually attracted to people after developing a deep emotional connection with them.

Romantic identity terms:

- **Heteroromantic**: Describes someone who is romantically attracted to people of the opposite sex.
- **Homoromantic**: Describes someone who is romantically attracted to people of the same sex.
- **Biromantic**: Describes someone who is romantically attracted to both men and women (or any two genders).
- **Panromantic**: Describes someone who is romantically attracted to people of all or many genders.
- **Aromantic**: Describes someone who is not romantically attracted to people of any sex.

Gender identity terms:

- **Transgender**: Describes someone who's gender identity does not match their biological sex.
- **Cisgender**: Describes someone who's gender identity does match their biological sex.
- **Genderqueer**: Describes someone who's sense of gender is different than the typical gender binary.
- **Genderfluid**: Describes someone who's gender identity fluctuates.
- **Bi-gender**: Describes someone who identifies with both genders.
- **Agender**: Describes someone who does not identify with either gender.

Other terms:

- **LGBTQIA+**: An acronym that stands for Lesbian, Gay, Bisexual, Transgender, Queer/Questioning, Intersex, Asexual/Ally, and other.
- **Queer**: An umbrella term that describes any identity that is not part of the norm.
- **Intersex**: Describes a person who's biological sex is not entirely male or female.
- **Ally**: A person who is not part of the LGBTQIA+ community but is accepting and supportive of the community.

Gender and sexuality and complex and each person's identity is unique to them. For more information about sexuality and gender, see the following resources.

Resources

WCU Intercultural Affairs and Safe Zone Program
227 AK Hinds University Center
828-227-2276
ica.wcu.edu
ica@wcu.edu or safezone@wcu.edu
Counseling and Psychological Services
225 Bird Building
828-227-7469
caps.wcu.edu
Sexuality and Gender Alliance (SAGA)
orgsync.wcu.edu
(Also on Facebook)

Sexual Violence Definitions

- **Sexual harassment**: Any unwelcome behavior of a sexual nature.
- **Sexual exploitation**: Exchanging sexual acts for some type of incentive, profit, or gain.
- **Sexual assault**: Umbrella term for any forced, unwanted sexual contact with a person against their will or by threat of force.
- **Rape**: Forced, unwanted sexual intercourse with a person against their will or by threat of force.
- **Stalking**: Harassment through unwanted/obsessive attention (following, watching, phone calls, texts, etc.).
- **Child sexual abuse**: Contact or interaction between a child and an adult in which the child is used for the sexual gratification or stimulation of the adult.
- **Consent**: Agreement to engage in a sexual activity.
  - ✓ Verbally giving, receiving, or withdrawing consent is safest because it is more clear than relying on nonverbal communication.
  - ✓ Can gain consent by asking questions like "Do you like that?" and "Is this ok?"
  - ✓ Assume there is *no consent* unless there is a clear and enthusiastic yes!

- **Victim blaming**: Accusing a victim of sexual assault of being partially or fully responsible for their assault.
  - ✓ Examples:
    - ○ "Why didn't you fight back?"
    - ○ "You shouldn't have been alone with the person. What did you think was going to happen?"
    - ○ "You were drunk. You probably said yes and don't remember."
    - ○ "You were dressed really provocatively. You were asking for it."
  - ✓ There are things that we all can do proactively to minimize our risk of being victimized, like being aware of our surroundings, using the "buddy system," and consuming alcohol only in moderation or not at all. Regardless of someone's choices though, it never gives someone the right to assault them. It is never the victim's fault!

Resources

WCU Campus Police

Emergencies: (828) 227-8911

Non Emergencies: (828) 227-7301

WCU Health Services

(828) 227-7640

WCU Counseling and Psychological Services

(828) 227-7469

Jackson County Department of Public Health

(828) 586-8994

REACH of Macon County

Macon Office (828) 369-5544

Jackson Office (828) 586-8969

© Boris15/Shutterstock.com

CHAPTER EIGHT
SUBSTANCE USE AND ABUSE

By: Gayle Wells

Introduction

The abuse of drugs and alcohol has become a life-threatening problem. For example, tobacco use is responsible for roughly 440,000 American deaths each year! Alcohol abuse is linked to an additional 88,000 deaths (Centers for Disease Control and Prevention [CDC], 2017).

Along with increasing the risks of disease, substance use and abuse can also inhibit brain function. A growing body of research is showing that substances such as nicotine, alcohol, and marijuana can impact brain function. Furthermore, many of these substances are either physically addictive, emotionally habituated, or both.

The human brain develops from back to front and is divided into three main levels: the vegetative brain, the emotional brain (limbic system), and the logic brain (neocortical level). The vegetative brain develops first followed by the emotional brain, and, finally, the logic brain. In fact, the executive functioning in the neocortical level of the brain is not fully developed until about age 25. That is important to think about because risky behaviors such as drugs and alcohol impact brain development. When teenagers and young adults use substances, brain development is affected.

© itakdalee/Shutterstock.com

Source: Centers for Disease Control and Prevention (CDC). 2017.

Alcohol Use and Your Health

Drinking too much can harm your health. Excessive alcohol use leads to about 88,000 deaths in the United States each year, and shortens the life of those who die by almost 30 years. Further, excessive drinking cost the economy $249 billion in 2010. Most excessive drinkers are not alcohol dependent.

What is considered a "drink"?

U.S. Standard Drink Sizes

(examples: gin, rum, vodka, whiskey)

12 ounces
5% beer

8 ounces
7% malt liquor

5 ounces
12% wine

1.5 ounces
40% (80 proof)
distilled spirits

Excessive alcohol use includes:

Binge Drinking

For women, 4 or more drinks consumed on one occassion

For men, 5 or more drinks consumed on one occassion

Heavy Drinking

For women, 8 or more drinks per week

For men, 15 or more drinks per week

Any alcohol used by pregnant women

Any alcohol used by those under the age of 21 years

If you choose to drink, do so in moderation:

FOR WOMEN, up to 1 drink a day

FOR MEN, up to 2 drinks a day

DON'T DRINK AT ALL if you are under the age of 21, or if you are or may be pregnant, or have health problems that could be made worse by drinking.

NO ONE should begin drinking or drink more frequently based on potential health benefits.

Excessive alcohol use has immediate effects that increase the risk of many harmful health conditions. These are most often the result of binge drinking. Over time, excessive alcohol use can lead to the development of chronic diseases and other serious problems.

Short-Term Health Risks

Injuries

- Motor vehicle crashes
- Falls
- Drownings
- Burns

Violence

- Homicide
- Suicide
- Sexual assault
- Intimate partner violence

Alcohol poisoning
Reproductive health

- Risky sexual behaviors
- Unintended pregnancy
- Sexually transmitted diseases, including HIV
- Miscarriage
- Stillbirth
- Fetal alcohol spectrum disorders (FASDs)

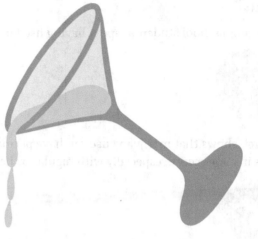

Long-Term Health Risks

Chronic diseases

- High blood pressure
- Heart disease
- Stroke
- Liver disease
- Digestive problems

Cancers

- Breast
- Mouth and throat
- Liver
- Colon

Learning and memory problems

- Dementia
- Poor school performance

Mental health

- Depression
- Anxiety

Social problems

- Lost productivity
- Family problems
- Unemployment

Alcohol dependence

http://www.cdc.gov/alcohol/fact-sheets/alcohol-use.htm

What You Need to Know About Marijuana Use and Teens

Fast Facts

- 38% of high school students report having used marijuana in their life.[1]

- Research shows that marijuana use can have permanent effects on the developing brain when use begins in adolescence, especially with regular or heavy use.[2]

- Frequent or long-term marijuana use is linked to school dropout and lower educational achievement.[3]

The teen years are a time of rapid growth, exploration, and onset of risk taking. Taking risks with new behaviors provides kids and teens the opportunity to test their skills and abilities and discover who they are. But, some risk behaviors—such as using marijuana—can have harmful and long-lasting effects on a teen's health and well-being.

Marijuana and the teen brain

Unlike adults, the teen brain is actively developing and often will not be fully developed until the mid 20s. Marijuana use during this period may harm the developing teen brain.

Negative effects include:

- Difficulty thinking and problem solving.
- Problems with memory and learning.
- Impaired coordination.
- Difficulty maintaining attention.[3]

Negative effects on school and social life

Marijuana use in adolescence or early adulthood can have a serious impact on a teen's life.

- **Decline in school performance.** Students who smoke marijuana may get lower grades and may more likely to drop out of high school than their peers who do not use.[4]
- **Increased risk of mental health issues.** Marijuana use has been linked to a range of mental health problems in teens such as depression or anxiety.[5] Psychosis has also been seen in teens at higher risk like those with a family history.[6]

- **Impaired driving.** Driving while impaired by any substance, including marijuana, is dangerous. Marijuana negatively affects a number of skills required for safe driving, such as reaction time, coordination, and concentration.[7, 8]
- **Potential for addiction.**[a] Research shows that about 1 in 6 teens who repeatedly use marijuana can become addicted, which means that they may make unsuccessful efforts to quit using marijuana or may give up important activities with friends and family in favor of using marijuana.

For more information, visit:

YRBSS Results, Slides, and MMWR Publications: https://www.cdc.gov/healthyyouth/data/yrbs/results.htm

Parent Engagement Tips: https://www.cdc.gov/healthyyouth/protective/parent_engagement.htm

School Connectedness: https://www.cdc.gov/ healthyyouth/protective/school_connectedness.htm

NIDA Drug Facts: Marijuana: https://teens.drugabuse.gov/drug-facts/marijuana

NIDA Marijuana: Facts for Teens: https://www.drugabuse.gov/publications/marijuana-facts-teens/letter-to-teens

Adolescents and Marijuana: http://learnaboutmarijuanawa.org/factsheets/adolescents.htm

References

[a]The term "addiction" is used to describe compulsive drug seeking despite negative consequences. However, we recognize that "addiction" is not considered a specific diagnosis in the fifth edition of The Diagnostic and Statistical Manual of Mental Disorders (DSM-5)—a diagnostic manual used by clinicians that contains descriptions and symptoms of all mental disorders classified by the American Psychiatric Association (APA). Rather the DSM-5 uses the term substance use disorder. However, throughout this document addiction is used synonymously with having a substance use disorder for ease of language recognition and understanding.

1. Centers for Disease Control and Prevention (CDC), High School Youth Risk Behavior Survey Data. 2016 [cited 2016 November 16, 2016]; Available from: http://nccd.cdc.gov/ youthonline/.

2. National Institute on Drug Abuse. What are marijuana's long-term effects on the brain? 2016 [cited 2016 November 16, 2016]; Available from: https://www.drugabuse.gov/publications/research-reports/marijuana/how-does-marijuana-use-affect-your-brainbody.

3. Fergusson, D.M. and J.M. Boden, Cannabis use and later life outcomes. Addiction, 2008. 103(6): p. 969-76; discussion 977-8.

4. Broyd, S.J., et al., Acute and Chronic Effects of Cannabinoids on Human Cognition-A Systematic Review. Biol Psychiatry, 2016. 79(7): p. 557-67.

5. Copeland, J., S. Rooke, and W. Swift, Changes in cannabis use among young people: impact on mental health. Curr Opin Psychiatry, 2013. 26(4): p. 325-9.

6. Arseneault, L., et al., Cannabis use in adolescence and risk for adult psychosis: longitudinal prospective study. BMJ, 2002. 325(7374): p. 1212-3.

7. Bondallaz, P., et al., Cannabis and its effects on driving skills. Forensic Sci Int, 2016. 268: p.92-102.

8. Hartman, R.L. and M.A. Huestis, Cannabis effects on driving skills. Clin Chem, 2013. 59(3): p. 478-92.

9. National Institute on Drug Abuse. Drugs, Brains, and Behavior: The Science of Addiction 2014 [cited 2016 December 29].

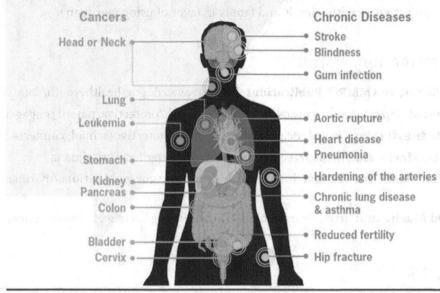

Risks from Smoking

Smoking can damage every part of the body

Cancers
- Head or Neck
- Lung
- Leukemia
- Stomach
- Kidney
- Pancreas
- Colon
- Bladder
- Cervix

Chronic Diseases
- Stroke
- Blindness
- Gum infection
- Aortic rupture
- Heart disease
- Pneumonia
- Hardening of the arteries
- Chronic lung disease & asthma
- Reduced fertility
- Hip fracture

Tobacco Industry Marketing

Cigarette and smokeless tobacco companies spend billions of dollars each year to market their products (Federal Trade Commission [FTC], 2016).

- In 2014, cigarette and smokeless tobacco companies spent more than $9 billion on advertising and promotional expenses in the United States alone (FTC, 2016).
- Cigarette companies spent approximately $8.49 billion on cigarette advertising and promotion in 2014, down from $8.95 billion in 2013 (FTC, 2016).
  - ✓ The five major U.S. smokeless tobacco manufacturers spent $600.8 million on smokeless tobacco advertising and promotion in 2014, an increase from $503.2 million spent in 2013 (FTC, 2016).

The money cigarette and smokeless tobacco companies spent in 2014 on U.S. marketing amounted to:

- Nearly $25 million each day (FTC, 2016)
- More than $28 for every person (adults and children) in the United States per year (according to 2014 population estimate of 320,000,000) (Census Bureau, 2016; FTC, 2016)
- More than $227 per year for each U.S. adult smoker (based on 40 million adult smokers in 2014) (CDC, 2014; FTC, 2016)

The following three categories totaled approximately $7.4 billion and accounted for 87% of all cigarette company marketing expenditures in 2014 (FTC, 2016):

- Price discounts paid to retailers or wholesalers to reduce the price of cigarettes to consumers—nearly $6.8 billion

- Promotional allowances paid to cigarette retailers, such as payments for stocking, shelving, displaying, and merchandising particular brands—$260.3 million
- Promotional allowances paid to cigarette wholesalers, such as payments for volume rebates, incentive payments, value-added services, and promotions—$363.3 million

Marketing to Specific Populations

Youth and Young Adults

Scientific evidence shows that tobacco company advertising and promotion influences young people to start using tobacco (U.S. Department of Health and Human Services [USDHHS], 2012).

- Adolescents who are exposed to cigarette advertising often find the ads appealing.
- Tobacco ads make smoking appear to be appealing, which can increase adolescents' desire to smoke.

The three most heavily advertised brands—Marlboro, Newport, and Camel—were the preferred brands of cigarettes smoked by adolescents (aged 12–17 yr) and young adults (aged 18–25 yr) during 2008–2010 (USDHHS, 2012).

Brand preferences of adolescents (USDHHS, 2012):

- 46.2% preferred Marlboro
- 21.8% preferred Newport
- 12.4% preferred Camel
- 16.0% preferred other brands
- 3.5% preferred no usual brand

Brand preferences of young adults (USDHHS, 2012):

- 46.1% preferred Marlboro
- 21.8% preferred Newport
- 12.4% preferred Camel
- 15.2% preferred other brands
- 1.6% preferred no usual brand

Women

Women have been targeted by the tobacco industry, and tobacco companies have produced brands specifically for women. Marketing toward women is dominated by themes of social desirability and independence, which are conveyed by advertisements featuring slim, attractive, and athletic models (National Cancer Institute [NCI], 2008; USDHHS, 2001).

Racial/Ethnic Communities

Advertisement and promotion of certain tobacco products appear to be targeted to members of racial/minority communities.

- Marketing to Hispanics and American Indians/Alaska Natives has included advertising and promotion of cigarette brands with names such as Rio, Dorado, and American Spirit (USDHHS, 1998, 2001).

- The tobacco industry has targeted African American communities in its advertisements and promotional efforts for menthol cigarettes. Strategies include (USDHHS, 2001, 2012):
  ✓ Campaigns that use urban culture and language to promote menthol cigarettes
  ✓ Tobacco-sponsored hip-hop bar nights with samples of specialty menthol cigarettes
  ✓ Targeted direct-mail promotions
- Tobacco companies' marketing to Asian Americans has included (USDHHS, 1998, 2001):
  ✓ Sponsorship of Chinese and Vietnamese New Year festivals and other activities related to Asian/Pacific American Heritage Month
  ✓ Heavy billboard and in-store advertisements in predominantly urban Asian American communities
  ✓ Financial and in-kind contributions to community organizations
  ✓ Support of Asian American business associations

References

Census Bureau. (2016). *Monthly population estimates for the United States: April 1, 2010 to December 1, 2016*. Washington, DC: U.S. Department of Commerce, Census Bureau (accessed December 19, 2016).

Centers for Disease Control and Prevention (CDC). (2014). Current cigarette smoking among adults—United States, 2005–2014. *Morbidity and Mortality Weekly Report, 64*(44), 1233–1240 (accessed December 19, 2016).

Centers for Disease Control and Prevention (CDC). (2017). *Alcohol and public health: Alcohol-related disease impact (ARDI). Average for United States 2006–2010 alcohol-attributable deaths due to excessive alcohol use*. Retrieved from https://nccd.cdc.gov/DPH_ARDI/Default/Report.aspx?T=AAM&P=f6d7eda7-036e-4553-9968-9b17ffad620e&R=d7a9b303-48e9-4440-bf47-070a4827e1fd&M=8E1C5233-5640-4EE8-9247-1ECA7DA325B9&F=&D=. (Accessed January 18, 2017).

Federal Trade Commission. (2016). *Federal trade commission cigarette report for 2014*. Washington, DC: Federal Trade Commission (accessed December 19, 2016).

National Cancer Institute. (2008). *The role of the media in promoting and reducing tobacco use*. Bethesda, MD: U.S. Department of Health and Human Services, National Institutes of Health, National Cancer Institute (accessed December 19, 2016).

U.S. Department of Health and Human Services. (1998). *Tobacco use among U.S. racial/ethnic minority groups—African Americans, American Indians and Alaska Natives, Asian Americans and Pacific Islanders, and Hispanics: A report of the surgeon general*. Atlanta, GA: U.S. Department of Health and Human Services, Centers for Disease Control and Prevention, National Center for Chronic Disease Prevention and Health Promotion, Office on Smoking and Health (accessed December 19, 2016).

U.S. Department of Health and Human Services. (2001). *Women and smoking: A report of the surgeon general*. Atlanta, GA: U.S. Department of Health and Human Services, Public Health Service, Centers for Disease Control and Prevention, National Center for Chronic Disease Prevention and Health Promotion, Office on Smoking and Health (accessed December 19, 2016).

U.S. Department of Health and Human Services. (2012). *Preventing tobacco use among youth and young adults: A report of the surgeon general*. Atlanta, GA: U.S. Department of Health and Human Services, Centers for Disease Control and Prevention, National Center for Chronic Disease Prevention and Health Promotion, Office on Smoking and Health (accessed December 19, 2016).

This document is from www.cdc.gov

CHAPTER NINE
OUTDOOR ACTIVITY

By: Bob Beaudet

© Alxcrs/Shutterstock.com

Introduction

Whether a person is engaged in a quiet stroll or working with a group to navigate a white-water river, outdoor recreation can provide multiple benefits. The benefits can be physical such as the reduction in heart disease gained from moderate exercise such as a brisk walk or off-road bike ride. The benefits may be gained through social activities such as participating in a round of disc golf or a team event such as Ultimate Frisbee. A person participating in outdoor activities can reduce stress levels, anxiety, and depression.

Western North Carolina provides outdoor opportunities that are second to none. Within a short car ride, a person can choose to participate in leisurely activities such as a quiet stroll in a national forest or gaze

Contributed by Bob Beaudet. Copyright © Kendall Hunt Publishing Company.

at a herd of elk in a national park. The activity can be of moderate intensity such as hiking along a wooded trail to view one of hundreds of waterfalls in the region. The activity can be more vigorous such as hiking along portions of the Appalachian Trail or riding a mountain bike through the Pisgah National Forest. Or the activity may be a group challenge such as rafting along the Nantahala or Pigeon River. The activity could be seasonal such as snow skiing in the winter or tubing the French Broad in the summer.

Students at Western Carolina University (WCU) are fortunate in that they have access to all of the abovementioned activities as well as resources right on campus. If they are in the mood for a hike or an off-road bike ride Western has a trail system right on campus. If they are in a competitive mood, there are intramural activities for all abilities and interests. Or if they would like to access the surrounding areas Base Camp Cullowhee will help with the adventure from equipment rental to providing transportation, equipment, and instruction for guided adventures.

Additional Resources

American Hiking Society | *americanhiking.org*

Blue Ridge Parkway Hiking Trails | *brptrails.com*

Friends of Panthertown | *panthertown.org*

Great Smoky Mountains National Park | *nps.gov/grsm/index.htm* Hiking in the Smokys | *hikinginthesmokys.com*

Hiking in Western North Carolina | *hikewnc.info*

Nantahala National Forest Hiking Trails | *ncnatural.com/NCUSFS/Nantahala/trails.html*

http://www.wcu.edu/WebFiles/PDFs/WheeHikingGuide_printable.pdf

© Monkey Business Images/Shutterstock.com

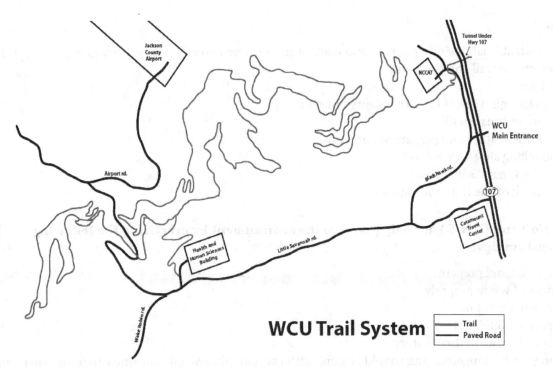

WCU Trail System

	Trail
	Paved Road

Source: Health and Physical Education Program at Western Carolina University. Reprinted with permission.

Hiking and Biking Tips

© inigocia/Shutterstock.com

Be Safe!!

- Hike with at least one other person and make sure someone knows where you are going
- Research the trail and the terrain
- Pack light
- Bring the right type of food and plenty of water
- Remember sunscreen!!
- Check the weather and prepare accordingly
- Good hiking shoes are a must
- Consider the risks involved
- Keep track of the time and your location

Leave No Trace (L.N.T.) and **help preserve the environment by practicing the following conservation tips:**

- Plan ahead and prepare
- Dispose of waste properly
- Leave what you find
- Respect wildlife
- Be considerate of other visitors
- Hiking can be dangerous and should be done with caution. Always tell someone where you are going and take extra water and clothing

To learn more visit *www.lnt.org*

Waterfall Safety

Waterfalls are popular places for viewing, picnicking, and wading. Although beautiful to see, they often pose risks to unprepared visitors.

Slippery rocks, steep slopes, and undercurrents can catch you by surprise when walking through or in the vicinity of a waterfall.

© MarkVanDylePhotography/Shutterstock.com

Safety Checklist

✓ Know the potential hazards of waterfalls
✓ Stay back from the edge
✓ Avoid slippery rocks
✓ Wear stable shoes and watch your footing. Don't jump off of waterfalls
✓ Don't swim in waterfall pools
✓ Stay out of restricted areas
✓ Always carry a map of the area
✓ Wear proper attire

https://www.fs.usda.gov/Internet/FSE_DOCUMENTS/stelprd3849288.pdf